International and Development Education

Series Editors

W. James Jacob
University of Pittsburgh
Pittsburgh, Pennsylvania, USA

John N Hawkins
Education Program, East West Center
Honolulu, Hawaii, USA

The International and Development Education series focuses on the complementary areas of comparative, international, and development education. Books emphasize a number of topics ranging from key international education issues, trends, and reforms to examinations of national education systems, social theories, and development education initiatives. Local, national, regional, and global volumes (single authored and edited collections) constitute the breadth of the series and offer potential contributors a great deal of latitude based on interests and cutting edge research. INTERNATIONAL EDITORIAL ADVISORY BOARD Clementina Acedo, Webster University, Switzerland Philip G. Altbach, Boston University, USA Carlos E. Blanco, Universidad Central de Venezuela Oswell C. Chakulimba, University of Zambia Sheng Yao Cheng, National Chung Cheng University, Taiwan Ruth Hayhoe, University of Toronto, Canada Yuto Kitamura, Tokyo University, Japan Wanhua Ma, Peking University, China Ka Ho Mok, Hong Kong Institute of Education, China Christine Musselin, Sciences Po, France Yusuf K. Nsubuga, Ministry of Education and Sports, Uganda Namgi Park, Gwangju National University of Education, Republic of Korea Val D. Rust, University of California, Los Angeles, USA Suparno, State University of Malang, Indonesia John C. Weidman, University of Pittsburgh, USA Husam Zaman, Taibah University, Saudi Arabia.

More information about this series at
http://www.springer.com/series/14849

Deane E. Neubauer • Catherine Gomes
Editors

Quality Assurance in Asia-Pacific Universities

Implementing Massification in Higher Education

palgrave
macmillan

Editors
Deane E. Neubauer
East-West Center
Asia Pacific Higher Education
Research
Honolulu, Hawaii, USA

Catherine Gomes
RMIT University
School of Media and Communication
Melbourne, Victoria, Australia

International and Development Education
ISBN 978-3-319-83443-6   ISBN 978-3-319-46109-0   (eBook)
DOI 10.1007/978-3-319-46109-0

This Palgrave Macmillan imprint is published by Springer Nature
The registered company is Springer International Publishing AG
The registered company address is: Gewerbestrasse 11, 6330 Cham, Switzerland

Acknowledgments

We would like to express our gratitude and appreciation to the team of organizers at Zhejiang University in Hangzhou, China, for arranging and providing the context for the seminar from which these chapters were developed. Zhejiang University is a member of the Asia Pacific Higher Education Research Partnership (APHERP), as are all the institutions with which the contributors are associated. In particular, we want to thank Professor Xu Xiaozhou, dean of the College of Education, and his excellent staff, for hosting the event.

We would also like to thank the staff of the East-West Center which serves as the secretariat for APHERP and who also contributed significantly to the arrangements for the seminar, in particular Penny Higa, Audrey Minei, and Cheryl Tokita. Ellen Waldrop who prepared the index also has our thanks. We would like to acknowledge the assistance of staff at Palgrave Macmillan for their continued support.

Finally, we would like to thank the contributors of this volume, whose tireless work in achieving and maintaining quality standards in their respective institutions is admirable and humbling.

Deane E. Neubauer
Catherine Gomes

Author Biographies

Abrizah Abdullah is a Professor in the Department of Library and Information Science, University of Malaya, since 2000. She is also the deputy dean of the Institute of Graduate Studies, University of Malaya, and a research fellow at the Malaysian Citation Centre, Ministry of Education, Malaysia. She holds a BSc (Hons) in Environmental Engineering from Temple University, Philadelphia, and obtained her master's and PhD degrees, both in Library and Information Science from the University of Malaya. Her research interests include digital libraries, information behavior, bibliometrics, and scholarly communication. She is the chief editor of the *Malaysian Journal of Library & Information Science* listed in the Social Science Citation Index (SSCI).

Valentina M. Abordonado received a BEd in Secondary Education in 1976 and an MEd in Secondary Education in 1983 from the University of Hawaii at Manoa and a PhD in Rhetoric, Composition, and the Teaching of English from the University of Arizona in 1998. Her career began as an ESL teacher and an ESL Resource Teacher for the Hawaii Public Schools. She then served as a USAF officer in various roles, such as Squadron Section Commander at Wheeler AFB, Hawaii, assistant professor of English at the USAF Academy, Colorado, and an executive officer at Kadena AB, Okinawa, Japan. During the last 17 years, she has served at Hawaii Pacific University as Professor of English, Writing Program Chair, Service Learning Program Chair, Teaching and Learning Center Director, School of Education Director, and, most recently, as Assistant Dean for General Education. She teaches English and education courses, and her research interests include curriculum, teaching, and assessment.

Pham Thi Bich has been Deputy Director of Center for Educational Testing and Quality Assessment, Viet Nam National University-Ho Chi Minh City, Vietnam, responsible for quality assurance in her university since 2013. She received her bachelor of science in Computational and Applied Mathematics at University of Sciences and a master's degree in Education at Vietnam National University, Hanoi, Vietnam. Her research interests include higher education, educational measurement, and quality assurance.

Karen Hui-Jung Chen is specialized in the research areas of evaluation in higher education, comparative education, and higher education policy. She has taught at the department of education in the National Taipei University of Education in Taiwan as Assistant Professor. She is the executive editor of the journal *Higher Education Evaluation and Development (HEED)*, which has published 18 issues in 9 years. She has been working as a research fellow of the Higher Education Evaluation and Accreditation Council of Taiwan, which is a national quality assurance agency in Taiwan.

Cathryn L. Dhanatya is Chief Administrative and Financial Officer and Scholar of Policy at the UCLA Williams Institute. In this capacity, she oversees all operations and research administration for the center. Previously, she was the USC Rossier School of Education's first Assistant Dean for Research. Prior to coming to Rossier in 2010, she was Director of Research and Financial Administration for the Art|Global Health Center at UCLA, where she became specially trained in issues related to international research administration, foreign taxation laws, and issues related to human subject research.Dhanatya holds a PhD in Social Science and Comparative Education from UCLA, and has conducted research on media and technology as it relates to health issues around the globe. She also was project manager on a number of HIV/AIDS, marriage equality, and transgender research advocacy projects throughout her career.

Fauza Ab. Ghaffar is Professor in Geography at the Faculty of Arts and Social Sciences, University of Malaya. She is the dean of Graduate Studies. Prior to the deanship, Ghaffar was the director of the Quality Management and Enhancement Centre (QMEC), an internal quality agency of the university. Ghaffar has been involved in the quality venture of the university since 2001 and played a pivotal role in the institutionalizing of the quality framework for the university. At the national level, she is on the panel of assessors for accreditation of institution and programs appointed by the Malaysian Qualification Agency (MQA). Since 2003, Ghaffar has also been actively involved in the ASEAN University Network Quality Framework as an assessor and a training facilitator. With her vast involvement in quality assessment at program level among universities of the ASEAN countries and the training of the AUN-QA framework across the AUN member universities, she has also been appointed as the expert consultant on AUN-QA by the QAU secretariat.

Catherine Gomes is a senior lecturer at RMIT University in Melbourne and recently completed an Australian Research Council DECRA (Discovery Early Career Research Award) fellowship. Her work covers migration, transnationalism and diasporas, particularly transient migration in Australia and Singapore and with a special interest in international students, their well-being, social networks and media and communication use. Gomes is founding editor of *Transitions: Journal of Transient Migration* (Intellect Books). Her recent books include *Multiculturalism through the Lens: A Guide to Ethnic and Migrant Anxieties in Singapore* (2015), *The Asia Pacific in the Age of Transnational Mobility: The Search for Community and Identity on and through Social Media* (2016), *Transient Mobility and Middle Class Identity: Media and Migration in Australia and Singapore* (Palgrave Macmillan, 2017) and *International Student Connectedness and Identity: Transnational Perspectives* (Springer, 2017).

Xiao Han is a PhD candidate in the Department of Asian and Policy Studies, Hong Kong Education University. Her research interests include transnational higher education, higher education policy, and education inequality.

Angela Yung Chi Hou is Professor of higher education at Fu Jen Catholic University and a Higher Education Evaluation & Accreditation Council of Taiwan (HEEACT) Research Fellow. She now serves as Dean of the Office of International Education of Fu Jen Catholic University and the Vice President of the Asia Pacific Quality Network (APQN). Currently, she is also in the service of chief-in-editor of *HEED Journal* jointly published by HEEACT and Asian Pacific Quality Network (APQN) and the associate editor of *Journal of Asian Pacific Educational Review (SSCI)*. Her special interests include higher education policy, quality management, internationalization, faculty development, and quality assurance of cross-border higher education.

Shangbo Li is a Professor at the Open University of China, Beijing, and specially appointed research fellow at J. F. Oberlin University, Tokyo. She specializes in higher education and Japanese studies. Currently, she is working on a book-length survey of comparative higher education.

Deane E. Neubauer is Emeritus Professor of Political Science at the University of Hawaii at Manoa (UHM). He holds a BA from the University of California, Riverside, and an MA and PhD from Yale University. He has long been interested in the conduct of policy within and between democratic nation states, an interest that has over time focused on comparative democratic institutions, policy processes, health care, food security, education, and, more recently, the development and conduct of globalization. He has taught at the University of California, Irvine (1965–1970), prior to taking a position at UHM. He was the founding dean of Social Sciences at UHM from 1981 to 1988, and in 1999, the founder of the Globalization Research Center and the Globalization Research Network, a collaboration of four US universities, positions he held through 2004. He has also served as Chancellor of UHM and as the Vice President for Academic Affairs for the ten-campus University of Hawaii system. From 2004 to 2012, he served as a consultant to the Education Program of the East West Center.Since 2013, he has been co-director of the Asia Pacific Higher Education Research Partnership. His current work examines the varieties of national policy expressions in health care, food security, and higher education within the contemporary dynamics of globalization with particular attention to nations in the Asia Pacific region.

Nguyen Thi Thanh Nhat is a researcher of Center for Educational Testing and Quality Assessment, an affiliated organization of Viet nam National University-Ho Chi Minh City (VNU-HCM). She obtained her bachelor degree in Oriental Studies from VNU-HCM University of Social Sciences and Humanities in 2003. After graduation, she worked for the Faculty of Oriental Studies, VNU-HCM University of Social Sciences and Humanities. She received her master degree in International Studies from the University of Leeds, England, in 2005. She started to work for the Center for Educational Testing and Quality Assessment, VNU-HCM, in 2009 and has been responsible for activities related to quality assessment at program level within the system since 2014. Her research interests center on education policy and higher education quality assurance.

Wen Huey Tsui is an Associate Professor in the Department of Life Science at Fu Jen Catholic University. She now serves as executive director of the Institutional Research Office and director of the center for Academic Development and Evaluation of Fu Jen Catholic University. She specializes in management of Ministry of Education subsidies for university development and evaluations of departments, institutes, and research centers.

Xiaojun Zhang is a lecturer in Higher Education Management at the Institute of Leadership and Education Advanced Development (ILEAD), Xi'an Jiaotong-Liverpool University, China. He also serves as the deputy director of ILEAD. He received his PhD from Xi'an Jiaotong University. His research focuses on future universities, indigenous leadership, institutional change, and the role of leadership in institutional change in higher education context. Zhang is also interested in HeXie (Harmony) Management theory which was proposed and developed by Chinese scholars. His work has appeared in *Leadership Quarterly*, *Journal of Organizational Change Management*, *Chinese Management Studies*, and many journals in Chinese.

Hong Zhu holds a PhD in Second Language Education from Ontario Institute for Studies in Education (OISE), University of Toronto, with a research interest focusing on recent immigrants from the People's Republic of China to Canada. Her dissertation, "Capital Transformation and Immigrant Integration: Chinese Independent Immigrants' (CIIs) Language Practices and Social Practices in Canada", is an ethnographic study on CIIs' integration experience in Canada. In addition to her own research on immigrant integration, Zhu participated in various research projects in the University of Toronto, such as SSHRC-funded projects University-Union Research on Socially Responsible Investigation of Pension Funds, Student Experiences in Toronto Classrooms, and Citizenship Learning and Participatory Democracy. In 2007, Zhu joined the faculty of education of Northeast Normal University (NENU) of China. In NENU, Zhu is the coordinator of the International Education Program for Post-graduate Degree in Education of NENU, which is the first full English education graduate program of China. Zhu teaches graduate courses, such as Research Methodology, Qualitative Inquiry, Curriculum Reform and Teacher Professional Development, and Language, Identity and Education. Both as the program coordinator and instructor, Zhu has been interested in international graduate students' adaptation in a full English instruction program in China. Currently, Zhu is working on an in-depth inquiry into international student identity in a new era of globalization.

Nneoma Grace L. Egbuonu is a third-year doctoral degree student in the field of Educational Economy and Management at Northeast Normal University, China. She is also an international student and has taught in the English program at the Faculty of Education at Northeast Normal University. Her research interests include international students' education and foreign language learning and acquisition, in addition to early childhood education. She has carried out research on foreign language learning at preschool level in China and has also worked in collaboration with lecturers and fellow international students to carry out research in the area of international students' education in China.

Contents

LIST OF FIGURES

LIST OF TABLES

CHAPTER 1

Creating Cultures of Quality Within Asia Pacific Higher Education Institutions

Deane E. Neubauer and Catherine Gomes

INTRODUCTION

Quality has been a central issue within higher education, of course, for many decades, having been a core element within the tradition of higher education accreditation throughout the twentieth century. However, with the massification of higher education over the past 40 years throughout the world, it has passed through numerous stages and variations as the elements within higher education that it attempted to define, measure and assess have themselves expanded in number and kind. Efforts to capture this variation and complexity have led to a defined literature primarily focused on the steps taken by such entities to establish and effect their varied criteria for review and to the significantly thorny issue of measurement (For some summary treatment of this, see Neubauer 2008). Such treatments of the quality issue tend to focus on how the formal entities

D.E. Neubauer (✉)
East-West Center, University of Hawaii,
Honolulu, HI, USA

C. Gomes
School of Media and Communication, RMIT University,
Melbourne, Australia

© The Author(s) 2017
D.E. Neubauer, C. Gomes (eds.),
Quality Assurance in Asia-Pacific Universities,
DOI 10.1007/978-3-319-46109-0_1

1

established to effect quality assurance operate and whether or not they are able to gain success in their varied operations.

What tends to be missing from this increasingly varied and diffuse reporting are studies that focus on how HEIs themselves engage issues of quality as an internal process that such institutions pursue in efforts to gain a measure of better self-understanding (as it were) of their own efforts. Throughout the reach of higher education wherever it is found, issues of quality arise and, with very modest inspection, prove to be marvelously complex and in many ways not a little puzzling—despite the fact that throughout the world quizzical minds of high quality and good intent continue to address the issue. In part, this situation arises because the notion of "quality" means many different things to many different people and in many different institutional contexts—which is to say that in a multitude of ways quality is situational—it means what it means to those addressing a given situation and circumstance. Yet, the *idea* of quality is familiar to us all: as Virginia Smith, the former president of Vassar used to say: "It may be hard to define it…but I *know it* when I see it." By which she also meant to imply, "and I know when it is absent from what I see."

Such a powerful intuitive sense of quality may serve individuals within the confines of a given program, or classroom, or faculty evaluation or even overall institutional assessment, but in the contemporary world of higher education massification, where the numbers of institutions, the numbers of students they serve and the complexity of the programs they invent and produce are all growing at unprecedented rates, far more effective precision is needed. And as we all know, this has been and continues to be the work in some way of all of higher education, made even more challenging by the increasing desire and need to develop comparative norms and measures that will allow some functional measure of comparability across a range of situations. These include, to name just a few, multiple institutions with differing missions within the same country as well as those that differ significantly in size and complexity; and even more daunting, those from different national settings and political jurisdictions throughout the world, including in growing numbers, those institutions that themselves purport to be transnational or global. As Simon Marginson has argued in various situations (including global ranking endeavors), increasingly the meaning and value of higher education as a process and a product constitute a "good", or a "value" within national and international (global) markets, and as with any "product" in any "market", higher education requires *a functional currency* in order for "us" to "know" what a degree, certificate or other higher education product is "worth" relative to others (Marginson and Sawir 2005; Neubauer 2011).[1]

In what follows, we establish a frame for discussing a variety of perspectives that involve various notions, understandings and practices of quality in Asia Pacific higher education. Our goal is to create a context that encourages readers to identify and inquire into a particular aspect of quality or an important dimension of quality that has become manifest within their own institution, country or transnational region. We do this not with any pretense that the result of such an exercise will prove comprehensive in any meaningful way, but that this framework may result in efforts to embody the insights and perhaps novel understandings of how quality (as a constantly dynamic and changing attribute) is being manifested, analyzed and, in many cases, measured within a range of specific institutions and historical contexts.

THE CONTEXT

Of the myriad examples one might choose to initiate this conversation, one that strikes us as having been particularly useful was that of the Global University Network for Innovation (GUNI) conference in 2006 on the subject: "Accreditation for Quality Assurance: What Is At Stake?" The very thoughtful and far-reaching papers in that conference (published simultaneously in a volume with the same title: GUNI 2006) retain much of their relevance today. Of striking durability is the effort of Sanyal and Martin to enumerate the core meanings of quality.

- Providing excellence
- Being exceptional
- Providing value for money
- Conforming to specifications
- Getting things right the first time
- Meeting customers' needs
- Having zero defects
- Providing added value
- Exhibiting fitness of purpose

(Martin and Syndal 2006, p 5.)

Our assertion is that virtually all efforts by quality assurance entities at whatever level, as well as efforts taken within HEIs, embody some understanding of and effort to achieve quality in one or more of these senses. As the GUNI work makes clear, it is useful to think of each of these as both a potentially useful dichotomy (the attribute meant to embody the concept is either present or absent), or more usefully as a continuum for which discrete indicators are sought to obtain some aspect of relative measurement for the attribute. Indeed, many higher education accreditation entities have developed metrics and rubrics to encourage the institutions they accredit to develop empirical referents for these attributes, which as the foregoing suggests are often at the conceptual level so vague as to defeat the potential notion of measurement. This also raises the predicament of "external" assessment versus or in alignment with "internal" assessment about which more will be said later (See, e.g., the WASC 2013 Handbook).

Efforts to develop useful understandings and measurement of quality within higher education contexts (as if the task were not difficult enough as it were) are further complicated by a broad range of structural factors that have emerged around and through the various dynamics and pathways of globalization and in the manifestations of massification. These often lead to a seemingly constant flow of forces of change throughout societies, some of which have affected higher education directly and some of which create a set of background factors that impinge on higher education's ability to pursue its various missions with effective modalities of performance across whatever levels of quality they are able to create and sustain. Among these (but certainly not exclusively) are:

- Privatization and the "incorporation movement". Privatization of higher education has long been a feature of many higher education systems (e.g. Japan, Korea, Philippines and the USA), but over the past several decades, one can observe a considerable expansion of the reach of private education as the dynamics of massification of higher education outstrip public resources to meet demand (Hawkins and Mok 2015).

- Changes in funding patterns and sources. Economic globalization has both initiated and facilitated the spread of neoliberalism, which at the government level creates arguments for reducing the relative scope of the public sector in relation to the private sector. The impacts on higher education have led in many environments to a relative decrease in government funding for private education and an overall cost-shift toward increased student tuitions (Marginson and van Der Wende 2009).

- Autonomy. One companion of neoliberal influences on higher education has been the movement to provide higher education systems with greater "autonomy" from previously controlling governmental ministries. In many instances, the exchange for greater autonomy over higher education development and administration has been the companion reduction in governmental financial support (e.g. Indonesia, Japan and the USA) (Varghese and Martin 2014).
- The rapid expansion of higher education in given environments. The rapid expansion of higher education throughout many Asian societies has been without historical parallel, as governments and societies have sought to create vastly expanded access to higher education as a necessary pathway to economic development and the ability to compete within the increasingly competitive global environment. As such efforts have continued to develop into the process now known familiarly as massification, an increasingly common concern has arisen over whether such vast extensions of purpose and capability are in fact sustainable over time, and it follows that within this discourse, the issue of quality is paramount (Neubauer and Tanaka 2011; Mok et al. 2016).
- The rise of national agencies dedicated to quality assessment. Throughout the 1980s and into the 1990s and beyond, quality assurance entities were developed across Asia both within individual countries and as regional and transnational phenomena. These were assisted in no small measure by the various activities of the United Nations Educational, Scientific and Cultural Organization (UNESCO) and its role both in developing the Chiba Principles and assisting in the establishment of the International Network for Quality Assurance Agencies in Higher Education (INQAAHE) and the Asia Pacific Quality Network (APQN). The result is a virtual ubiquity of higher education quality assurance endeavors throughout the region, albeit with significant differences among them in terms of the concepts they employ to assert quality, the tools they employ to measure them and the policy consequences that flow across and within different countries from their operation. Once again, these intense external/national and international endeavors are increasingly bumping up against individual higher education institutional quality assurance policies and practices within or internal to the institutions themselves (e.g. See Hou 2014).
- Diversification of higher education systems. With massification and the expansions of capacity and the endeavors that have accompa-

nied them has come the creation and diversification of such systems themselves. It may be that the generalization holds "the larger the system" the more diversified and complex it is (e.g. China and India), but it may also hold that even within smaller systems, diversity of structure, function and outputs may depend on factors of particular meaning to the historical development of that particular system. Such would certainly be the case with the distinctive role played by private non-profit HEIs in the USA, which were created in a historical period that actually predated that of what would become the dominant state form of public higher education. The Philippines would be another example as the complex development of public and private institutions, especially those with a religious basis, owes much to borrowing from "without" as it does to the particularities of politics and social differentiation within the Philippines itself. The critical point here is that massification is a complex blending of common and unique factors that need to be considered contextually, and, to some extent, the meaning of quality is ultimately dependent on those contexts (Mok et al. 2016).

- Curricula changes and "alignment" issues. As HEIs become increasingly affected by the various dynamics of globalization (especially those that impact how societies, governments and their economies make resources available for higher education) the nature, shape and meanings embedded in curricula change also begin to change. If one can make a generalization about the current state of macro-curricular change in higher education, it is that the tying of higher education to national economies and HEIs' role in promoting innovation privileges Science, Technology, Engineering and Mathematics (STEM)-related fields (especially in graduate education) and all their endeavors over other parts of the curriculum. This continuously shifting set of emphases within institutions affects how quality is both conceived and sought to be implemented across different segments of such institutions (See, Hawkins et al. 2016).[2]

- Proliferation of multi-campus systems. Massification often results in the creation of multi-campus higher education structures, and with this structural arrangement, often come new challenges across a wide range of issues, not the least of which are the relationships that need to be established throughout the system to that entity viewed as at the top of the decision-making hierarchy. Such issues can include differences of mission between members of the system and relationships between system members themselves. Issues of quality are complicated because to some degree the "responsibility" for quality outcomes is placed within the campus context (especially in the USA where institutional accreditation is the norm), but in many ways is depedent on structures, rules, procedures and resources that extend behond individual campuses. (Wu and Wu 2013; Timberlake 2004; see also Douglass 2016).

- Online providers and the proliferating modalities of online education. Many voices are suggesting that the various modalities of online education will continue to rapidly develop over the next decade with the result that what had begun as the "disrupting movement" just a handful of years ago debuted as the year of the Massive Online Open Course (MOOC) in 2011–12 and has gained a new threshold of viability with the increasing cost of in-place education, and the question of sustainability of higher education in its traditional forms will transform into new, hybrid forms of higher education. As these do, they will perforce generate new demands for conceptual reconsideration of quality within higher education and equally innovative concepts and mechanisms of assessment and quality review (See, e.g., Christensen et al. 2011 and DeMillo 2015).

- Efforts to develop international standards for quality assurance. As education increasingly becomes more global, it has produced constant pressures for forms of quality assurance and quality measurement that can span the range of global differences and, at the same time, be sensitive to the novel modalities that continue to arise within higher education. As indicated above, regional quality assurance associations have sought to address the premise that the expansion of quality notions will remaining relevant within both local and regional quality constructs such as those built into evaluation frameworks. However, increasingly, it has seemed necessary to seek to create a common framework on which such regional and national efforts might be arranged, or at the very least which could inform them. Such as been the recent effort of the Council on Higher Education Accreditation's International Quality Group (CIGC) to do just this (CHEA 2016). This, we suspect will be but the first of many steps in the coming year to see some sort of "over-ordinating context developed which can continue to frame this dynamic and constantly changing international quality environment." (For a brief statement of the principles, see Appendix A).

Quality Issues Within the Context

Our intention in outlining these elements of a generalized "context" for contemporary higher education across international situations and borders has been to underscore the point that irrespective of how higher education quality assurance activities are framed, made explicit and placed within an operational context, we are suggesting that there exists a "continuous" context that has implications for obtaining measurement regimes and assessment measurements, as well as implications for the locus of quality assurance (institution professional association, governmental body, public agency, etc.)—the net result being a continual tension and interplay between HEI self-assessment and external agencies. And, it is both obvious and important to note that different institutions operating within different sub-contexts will experience such inputs and forces and respond to them within the immediate frames of reference within which such institutions exist. Thus, to return to our opening point, it is not only the overall effort to define and measure quality that is daunting, but it is also the effort to do this within these larger contextual frames of reference within which any given institution must operate.

And yet, HEIs do continue to operate in this assessment environment in a variety of particular and innovative ways. A highly varied process of quality assurance not only exists but also has grown in scope and density over the past several decades. This has been especially the case as the particular challenges of seeking to measure and assure higher education quality across borders becomes an ever-greater challenge with the continuous growth of cross-border education and with the emergence of international and global higher education institutional partnerships.

The chapters that appear in this volume were initially framed and given context in a "senior seminar" conducted by the Asia Pacific Higher Education Research Partnership (APHERP) held at Zhejiang University, Hangzhou, China, May 18–20, 2015. While inviting participants, we asked them to look inward to their own institutions, or others known to them, to identify and describe efforts that are taken at the institutional level to identify, describe and analyze instances of quality invention and improvement. The motive for this comes from numerous conversations that the editors have had within higher education accreditation and quality assurance contexts and outside it seeking to identify, develop, perpetuate and (in the words of many accreditation documents) seek methods of continuous quality improvement.

In short, we seek in this volume to explore the many different ways that quality issues are perceived, discussed and pursued among our participating institutions or those known to our participants. What does quality mean in the context of a given institution, and what does that institution do to create it, ensure and assure it and render it demonstrable to others? (Especially in the eyes of those who may come from outside the institution to seek and measure it!) How, for example, are quality issues discussed *within* a given institutional context and then made part of the regularized activities of that institution? How, to take another example, might individual efforts to create "quality moments" within a given educational program (perhaps, e.g., through the introduction of freshmen seminars, or the options for some—all?—students to pursue a "do-it-yourself" [DYI] experience, etc.) be reviewed, evaluated and generalized through the broader curriculum?

We are all perhaps quite familiar with how quality assurance is pursued by external agency accreditation and assessment, usually through a centralized body such as a ministry of education of some variety. In this seminar, we sought papers that would focus on the general question of "how is quality generated and maintained at the *institutional level?*" We recognize that the many institutions represented within APHERP are significantly different and see this as a virtue. We encouraged participants to bring to the seminar a range of experiences that may help to educate and inform their colleagues. We also hoped that in developing such papers participants could be sensitive to the various meanings of quality that emerge within these different institutional contexts, or the particular ways in which such institutions have themselves been affected by events within the more macro contextual levels that we have briefly described above.

Some areas, topics and issues relevant to *internal* institutional review that are illustrative of the kinds of issues that may be touched on in such a review include:

- Personnel review (faculty, department administrators, division administrators, vice chancellors [or vice presidents] and CEOs–presidents, chancellors, provosts etc.)
- Faculty recruitment, review, retention and dismissal—Who does it? How often? Checks and balances and so on.
- Academic program review (How often? How is it conducted? Rewards, sanctions etc.)
- Overall institutional review—role of faculty, students, administrators, outside stakeholders and peer review.

- Alignment of decentralized internal review by the HEIs, with more centralized external review often at the ministry level—what value is added to quality by these two levels of review? (Hawkins 2011).

These topics were meant to be illustrative only, but the goal was to provide some illumination of the dynamics, tensions, predicaments and future trajectories of these two approaches to quality assurance.

In Chapter 2, Angela Hou, Wen huey Tsui and Karen Hui-Jung Chen document how Taiwan, within a few short years, succeeded in a collective effort to establish a national quality assurance agency with the creation of the Higher Education Evaluation and Accreditation Council of Taiwan (HEEACT) as a joint effort between government and 153 colleges and universities. In its first iteration of institutional assessment, it reviewed institutions on a conventional basis, but beginning in 2013, the Ministry of Education (MOE) launched an initiative aimed at enhancing institutional autonomy as well as promoting an institution's own quality initiatives resulting in the process of self-accreditation. Within the first cycle of self-accreditation, 34 recipients of Taiwan's teaching and research excellence programs were asked to take part in this initiative. Hou et al. contribute a review of the progress of this initiative within Fu Jen Catholic University which as a member of this cohort initiated its own self-accreditation project in the spring of 2014. Within the context of the framework of this volume, such efforts at national self-accreditation are in part designed to promote institutional-sensitive and particular frameworks of quality that in part promote buy-in by all segments of a higher education institution.

A quite different approach to developing internal quality assessment mechanisms are detailed by Pham Thi Bich in Chap. 6 in documenting such efforts within the large and complex structure of Viet Nam National University-Ho Chi Minh City (VNU-HCM) which is an umbrella institution with six member universities, one separate faculty and a number of research institutions. The internal quality system developed (IQA) is designed to operate at three separate but linked levels, the VNU-HCM level, the institutional level and the departmental level. Within this system, VNU-HCM places emphasis on the operation of assessment at the program level, which assists in developing an internal quality culture. In the overall pattern of assessment, such program level activities are supplemented by reviews from external faculty from other VNU-HCM units, external HEIs within Vietnam and international participants. The intention throughout this system is to continuously create a comparative and growing culture of quality that can have demonstrable instances which can be shared within the overall university structure.

In a similar instance of an Asian university seeking to develop novel programs that will articulate a growing culture of quality, Hong Zhu details an innovative program developed at "North University" (a pseudonym) to teach English for international students while also constructing an interactive, cooperative community. Whereas the institution had delivered international programs in Chinese for many years, providing a full graduate program to students from five continents created an entirely new context for the faculty. Hong Zhu's study highlights the manner in which institutions are forced to adopt a "high internal learning culture" to make this transition, which she also cites as an instance of how individual institutions within a common quality and regulatory framework can create individual initiatives within a common quality regulatory context. In a somewhat related instance within the China context, Xiao Han and Xiaojun Zhang examine the possibilities that exist within the overall China regulatory framework for innovation and differentiation, in this instance choosing a Sino-foreign cooperation university as the case study. They have found that the university is able to operate within the conventional structures of quality assurance and to reach significantly beyond them to employ a range of techniques and practices to both meet the regulatory framework and reach far beyond it. In this instance, the payoff for University C is the ability to successfully place a significant number of its graduates in desirable admissions with foreign universities. Interestingly, University C has converted what might in other circumstances appear to be a burden, namely having to meet the regulatory requirements appropriate both to a domestic university and to the targeted assessments of its partner university, to forge a complex assessment of teaching and research quality which has allowed it to overall achieve high levels of both research and teaching qualities.

In Chaps. 7 and 8, respectively, Shangbo Li and Fauza Ab Ghaffar and A. Abrizah suggest how institution-specific instances of quality invention and pursuit may take place within relatively rigid QA procedures as mandated by strong national governmental agencies. At Japan's J. F. Oberlin University, Li suggests that the overall framework of quality has resulted in a complex local structure within the university that provides multiple levels of feedback to the teaching staff as well as from their designated research units. Faculty development committees also convene workshops for a variety of issues relevant to a constantly changing faculty mission in a university that increasingly focuses on educating both international students and Japan students from an internationally rich perspective. Working through a faculty development center, these engagements are focused in a variety of symposia each year to address additional subjects while assisting faculty in keeping the curriculum relevant and up to date. Within Malaysia, Ghaffar and Abrizah assert in Chap. 8 that the quality movement that encompasses major universities has entered a new stage as nationally, the Malaysian Qualifications Agency (MQA) has developed a complex system based strongly on international models. Within this system, not unlike that in Taiwan, the goal of leading institutions has been to work their way through standard review processes to gain the status of being self-accredited. This is the status reported on by Ghaffar and Abrizah at the University of Malaya, the nation's first and oldest HEI. Having made the point, the authors then turn to the important question of whether the university has merely achieved a sufficient measure of quality assurance to meet this standard or whether it has also been able to create a quality culture.

This notion of how quality comes to constitute a culture within an institution is focused on as well by Cathryn Dhanatya in Chap. 3 who poses the question in the context of strategic planning at a major US university. When done properly, she argues, strategic planning can be a central element in the quality process by virtue of its capacity to internally access processes and outcomes within institutions and to reflect "how each organization defines success which also relates to conversations of the development of quality products and services". Critically, as is frequently acknowledged, strategic planning exercises fall short of this goal and fail to make much headway in promoting both the understanding and the acceptance of a culture of quality in an institution, and seemingly the larger the institution, the more likely this is to be the case. Dhanatya provides a case study that argues for the contrary proposition as she examines an extensive strategic planning engagement of the Rossier School of Education at the University of Southern California, one of America's premier research institutions. The manner in which this instance of strategic planning has been developed and implemented at Rossier, she argues, ensures not only that a culture of quality is attenuated and given salience within the school, but also of equal value is the degree to which the outcomes featured in the plan link the school to its surrounding community (ies) by articulating a set of goals that can continue to form and lead the school in this task. The eventual outcome, she asserts, is that the strategic plan becomes a continuing instrument in an iterative process that frames virtually all the work that is done within the school, as it serves as well to attenuate processes of continued quality inquiry.

This model of diverse dimensions along which to pursue a course in the complex, multi-cultural area, that is Los Angeles, is echoed in the case study of Hawai'i Pacific University (HPU), a private higher education institution itself located in the culturally complex and rich environment of urban Honolulu. Developed to be an institution that would equally attract both "local" students from Hawai'i as well as significant numbers of international students (many from northern Europe), the issue of how to develop a quality culture became co-dimensional with the notion of how the university could equally navigate toward a culturally sensitive and responsive curriculum. In Chap. 9, Valentina M. Abordonado documents how HPU employed an Ishikawa Circle model to develop a "systematic, process-focused approach to planning, doing, studying and acting" to move toward the articulation of what such a quality culture would "look like" in this specific context and how it could be situated and implemented within the institution. Interestingly, in this particular context, the most promising approach appeared to be to work within the context of a new general education program being adopted by the institution (in part in response to its own external quality agency, the Western Association of Schools and Colleges) which sought to place cultural diversity itself at the center of this endeavor. In this process, part of the meaning of quality came to be represented through the range of cultural diversity represented within the curriculum. From this particular point of view of what the distinct "value-added component" of the general education program could and would be, the institution was able to integrate a wide range of methodological and pedagogic approaches within the curriculum, combined with an emphasis on interdisciplinary learning experiences and multiple team-taught courses. For HPU, the conventional notion of "whole person education" has taken a particular form by placing it within the overall context of cultural diversity as a distinctive element of programmatic quality.

The challenge of seeking identifiable and distinctive vectors for quality within distinct institutional contexts that are typified by cultural difference is addressed by Catherine Gomes in the concluding country study in this volume. As Australia faces the significant challenges laid out by its National Strategy for International Education, the country's higher education institutions face the significant challenge of sizable increases of international students from beyond their traditional markets in China,

India and Southeast Asia as they seek additional numbers of students from new and diverse international backgrounds, including Latin America and the Middle East. Gomes seeks to examine the novel challenges faced by Australia's higher education providers as they endeavor to accommodate such a sizable increment of culturally diverse students within an overall structure for international students of acknowledged quality throughout the world. Gomes points to the institutions that exist within the contemporary governing structure that provide an effective framework for developing both the capacity and the quality context for accommodating such a challenge.

We end this volume with an effort at concept formation in which Neubauer and Gomes suggest a typology of useful methods within institutions for pursuing effective quality activities and create a set of indicators that may be employed within higher education settings to help translate the broader, thematic statements of quality and excellence that are framed and transmitted by external quality assurance entities.

NOTES

1. Which, of course, is just where rankings come into the equation.
2. Note the action taken in 2015 by the Japanese government through its national education system to downgrade the role of humanities within national universities. Sawa 2015.

APPENDIX A

Context

The growing international activity within higher education—greater student mobility, expanding faculty exchanges and research collaboration, more cross-border partnerships among institutions and the growing reliance on online or Web-based education—has created a sense of urgency for a shared understanding of educational quality. While any single worldwide regimen of educational quality would be difficult and perhaps undesirable, a shared understanding about the dimensions of quality would be useful. These guiding principles are one effort to move toward such understanding while acknowledging and respecting the many differences of history, culture, beliefs and values that shape our systems of higher education and our perspectives on quality.

Purpose

The guiding principles are intended to serve as a framework for international deliberation about quality in higher education. Their aim is to seek common ground and establish a foundation for understanding quality. The principles may be used to inform discussions of quality, quality assurance and qualifications at the country, regional or international level.

The intended audiences include academics and other higher education professionals, students, employers, government officials and the public. They are invited to affirm and use these principles in the ongoing quest for effectiveness and quality in higher education

Principles

- Quality and higher education providers: Assuring and achieving quality in higher education is the primary responsibility of higher education providers and their staff.
- Quality and students: The education provided to students must always be of high quality whatever the learning outcomes pursued.
- Quality and society: The quality of higher education provision is judged by how well it meets the needs of society, engenders public confidence and sustains public trust.
- Quality and government: Governments have a role in encouraging and supporting quality higher education.
- Quality and accountability: It is the responsibility of higher education providers and quality assurance and accreditation bodies to sustain a strong commitment to accountability and provide regular evidence of quality.
- Quality and the role of quality assurance and accreditation bodies: Quality assurance and accreditation bodies, working with higher education providers and their leadership, staff and students, are responsible for the implementation of processes, tools, benchmarks and measures of learning outcomes that help to create a shared understanding of quality.
- Quality and change: Quality higher education needs to be flexible, creative and innovative; developing and evolving to meet students' needs, to justify the confidence of society and to maintain diversity. (Uvalic-Trumbic, 2016)

References

CHEA. (2016). *CHEA International Quality Group international quality principles.* Available at: http://www.chea.org/pdf/Quality%20Principles.pdf. Accessed 27 Dec 2016.

Christensen, C. M., Horn, M. B., Caldera, L., & Soares, L. (2011). *Disrupting college: How disruptive innovation can deliver quality and affordability to postsecondary education.* Center for American Progress/Innosight Institute. Available at: https://www.americanprogress.org/issues/economy/reports/2011/02/08/9034/disrupting-college/. Accessed 27 Dec 2016.

Demillo, R. (2015). *Revolution in higher education: How a small band of innovators will make college accessible and affordable.* Cambridge, MA: The MIT Press.

Douglass, J. A. (2016). *The New Flagship University: Changing the paradigm from global ranking to national relevancy.* New York: Palgrave Macmillan.

Hawkins, J. N. (2011). Higher education and quality assurance—Views from the inside and outside. In R. Yamada & R. Mori (Eds.), *Quality assurance for higher education and assessment.* Kyoto: Doshisha University.

Hawkins, J. N., & Mok, K. H. (Eds.). (2015). *Research, development, and innovation in Asia Pacific higher education.* New York: Palgrave Macmillan.

Hawkins, J. N., Neubauer, D., & Buasuwan, P. (2016). Situating graduate education in a rapidly changing higher education environment. In D. Neubauer & P. Buasuwan (Eds.), *Changing aspects of graduate education in the Asia Pacific region.* New York: Palgrave Macmillan.

Hou, A. (2014). Quality in cross-border higher education and challenges for the internationalization of national quality assurance agencies in the Asia-Pacific region: The Taiwanese experience. *Studies in Higher Education, 39*(1), 135–152.

Marginson, S., & Sawir, E. (2005). Interrogating global flows in higher education. *Globalization, Societies and Education, 3*(3), 281–309.

Marginson, S., & van der Wende, M. C. (2009). The new global landscape of nations and institutions. In Centre for Educational Research and Innovation (Ed.), *Higher education to 2030, Vol. 2: Globalization.* OECD.

Martin, M., & Syndal, B. C. (2006). Quality assurance and the role of anitation: An overview. In *Global University Network for Innovation* (pp. 3–23). *Accreditation for quality assurance: What is at stake?* Barcelona: GUNI. Also available at: http://www.guninetwork.org/guni.conference/2006_guni-conference. Accessed 7 Mar 2015.

Mok, K. H., Neubauer, D., & Jiang, J. (Eds.). (2016). *The sustainability of higher education in the Asia Pacific.* London: Routledge.

Neubauer, D. (2008). U.S. higher education accreditation old and new: The emergence of a new paradigm. *Evaluation in Higher Education, 2*(2), 23–49.

Neubauer, D. (2011). How might university rankings contribute to quality assurance endeavors? *Quality in Higher Education*, co-editor with J. Hawkins & T. DeMott. Available at: http://publications.apec.org/publication-detail. php?pub_id=1204. August 2011.

Neubauer, D., & Tanaka, Y. (Eds.). (2011). *Access, equity and capacity in Asia Pacific higher education*. New York: Palgrave Macmillan.

Sawa, T. (2015). Humanities under attack. *The Japan Times*. Available at: http://www.japantimes.co.jp/opinion/2015/08/23/commentary/japan-commentary/humanities-attack/#.VxV8zBhPmKw. Accessed 18 Apr 2016.

Timberlake, G. R. (2004). Decision-making in multi-campus higher education institutions. *The Community College Enterprise*, (Fall), Vol. 1, 91–99.

Uvalic-Trumbic, S. (2016). *The CIQC International Quality Principles: Toward a shared understanding of quality*. Washington, DC: CHEA. Available at: http://www.chea.org/pdf/Principles_Papers_Complete_web.pdf. Accessed 18 Apr 2016.

Varghese, N. V., & Martin, M. (2014). *Governance reforms in higher education: A study of institutional autonomy in Asian countries*. UNESCO: Institutional Institute for Educational Planning. Available at: http://unesdoc.unesco.org/images/0022/002272/227242e.pdf. Accessed 18 Apr 2016.

Wu, Y., & Wu, Z. (2013). Management of multi-campus universities in America and it enlightenment on Chinese multi-campus universities. *International Conference on Education Technology and Management Science*, (ICETMS 2013), 1338–1341.

PART I

Country Examples

Development of the Self-Accrediting System in Taiwan and Its Impact on Higher Education Institutions: A Case Study of Fu Jen Catholic University

Angela Yung Chi Hou, Wen Huey Tsui,
and Karen Hui-Jung Chen

INTRODUCTION

Over the past decade, all Asian nations have developed their own quality assurance system by setting up a national accreditor whose principal role is to accredit local tertiary education institutions and academic programs,

A.Y.C. Hou (✉)
Graduate Institute of Educational Leadership and Development, Fu Jen Catholic University,
Sinjhuang City, New Taipei City, Taiwan

W.H. Tsui
Office of Research and Development, Fu Jen Catholic University,
Sinjhuang City, New Taipei City, Taiwan

K.H.-J. Chen
Department of Education, National Taipei University of Education,
Taipei City, Taiwan

© The Author(s) 2017
D.E. Neubauer, C. Gomes (eds.),
Quality Assurance in Asia-Pacific Universities,
DOI 10.1007/978-3-319-46109-0_2

21

including Taiwan. Over the past 40 years, the number of Taiwan universities and colleges increased to 160 accounting for more than 1.3 million student enrollments, which has successfully transformed the Taiwan Higher Education system from an elite type into a universal type. Concurrently, quality issues related to "massification" in higher education have not only aroused public concerns but also resulted in the development of centralized system of quality assurance in Taiwanese higher education in the early twentieth century.

A version of quality assurance did not exist until a national accreditor, the Higher Education Evaluation and Accreditation Council of Taiwan (HEEACT), was established in 2005 with funds from the government and 153 colleges and universities. Prior to the establishment of HEEACT, several self-funded local accreditors had been founded, including the Taiwan Assessment and Evaluation Association (TWAEA), the Taiwan Medical Accreditation Council (TMAC), the Taiwan Nursing Accreditation Council (TNAC), and the Institute of Engineering Education Taiwan (IEET). In order to strengthen the international outlook and global competitiveness of Taiwan's colleges and universities, the Ministry of Education (MOE) has internationalized Taiwan's higher education with several polices, including encouraging universities to seek international accreditation (Hou 2011).

As a national accreditor, HEEACT operates both institutional and program-based accreditation. The external review costs are completely covered by the MOE. The detailed final reports are published on HEEACT's official website (HEEACT 2016). In 2006, HEEACT began a five-year cycle of program-based and nation-wide accreditation. The standards developed in the first cycle of program accreditation are as follows: (1) goals, features, and self-enhancement mechanisms; (2) curriculum design and teaching; (3) learning and student affairs; (4) research and professional performance; and (5) performance of graduates. There are three types of accreditation outcomes, including "Accredited", "Accredited Conditionally", and "Denial" (HEEACT 2012). According to HEEACT, the average rate in the first cycle for accredited status among a total of 1870 programs is 86 percent, for conditionally accredited 11.84 percent, and for denied status 1.97 percent (HEEACT 2012).

Starting in 2011, HEEACT conducted a new series of comprehensive assessments of over 81 four-year national and private universities and also continued the second cycle of program accreditation. Following the global trend of quality assurance, both institutional and programmatic accreditation focused on the assessment of student learning outcomes. The 2011 HEEACT's handbook of institutional accreditation emphasized that an institution would be evaluated and examined according to a Plan-Do-Check-Act (PDCA) model and an evidence-based assessment. Within this framework, each institution would first need to have a clear mission to state its institutional identity; second, it should have a favorable governance structure to integrate and allocate resources; and third, it should have set up a mechanism to assess student learning outcomes (HEEACT 2011). This second cycle of program accreditation in 2012 stressed the aim of realizing the development and operation of student learning outcomes evaluation mechanisms within programs and disciplines. The new accreditation model has been adopted specifically to assist universities in analyzing their strengths and weaknesses in facilitating successful student learning. The new standards for the second cycle of program accreditation covered the following areas: (1) educational goals, features, and curriculum design; (2) teaching quality and learning assessment; (3) student guidance and learning resources; (4) academic and professional performance; and (5) alumni performance and self-improvement mechanism (HEEACT 2012). Generally speaking, universities and programs were encouraged to develop measurable learning outcomes, to develop a variety of assessment tools at the course, program and institutional level, and to establish whether these learning outcomes are met. According to HEEACT, the pass rate of the second cycle program accreditation was up to 98.3 percent in the academic year of 2013 (HEEACT 2014).

In 2013, the MOE launched a new policy of self-accreditation, which aimed at enhancing institutional autonomy as well as promoting an institution's internal quality mechanism. Thirty-four recipients of Taiwan's Teaching and Research Excellence Programs were invited to take part in the new initiative. As a self-accrediting institution, Fu Jen started its self-accreditation process in April, 2014, and completed on-site visits and final reports by the end of the year. Hence, the main purpose of this chapter is to examine the new development of self-accreditation and its impact on Taiwan higher education and to demonstrate in specific how Fu Jen has moved to develop its own culture of quality as a result. Fu Jen is presented as a case study to realize these changes in the new system at the end of the chapter.

DEVELOPMENT OF A SELF-ACCREDITATION SYSTEM

According to The International Network for Quality Assurance Agencies in Higher Education (INQAAHE), self-accreditation is "a process or status that implies a degree of autonomy, on the part of an institution or individual, to make decisions about academic offerings or learning" (INQAAHE 2013). Self-accreditation derived from accreditation is defined as the status accorded to a mature institution conducting its Institutional Quality Assessment (IQA) and which is exempted from the process of external accreditation (Harvey 2014). In other words, self-accrediting universities are given autonomy to either award degrees in their own name or accredit their own programs without going through an external party. A self-accreditation institution is fully authorized to invite its review panel to inspect institutional or program quality. With greater familiarity with the specific nature of the institution itself, ideally, self-accreditation can lead institutions to a more informed process of self-improvement (Sanyal and Martin 2007; Kinser 2011). Hence, the main purpose of self-accreditation is to develop a quality culture on campuses throughout a rigorous internal quality review process by universities.

Self-accreditation tends to apply with a "fitness for purpose" approach only, inspecting how a university's performance fulfills its specific missions. Within a well-developed internal quality assurance system, institutional capacity will be also enhanced in order to deal with more complicated quality issues, such as program restructuring, faculty development, and so on (Stensaker et al. 2011). With an emphasis on self-enhancement, self-accreditation focuses more on development of internal quality assurance rather than external review.

Self-accreditation initially began in the UK and more recently has been adopted and implemented by some Asian countries, including Australia, Hong Kong, and Malaysia (TEQSA 2013a; MQA 2012; Wong 2013). In the UK, universities with a Royal Charter will be able to offer their own degrees. It means that these universities are "self-accrediting" institutions, though the term is not used often in the UK. Most of them are public universities, exemplified by the University of Cambridge having been the first Royal Charter University. Recently, self-accrediting status "has been applied to further education colleges that have been granted the right by The Privy Council to award its own foundation degrees" (INQAAHE 2013). In Australia, both self-accrediting and the non-self-accrediting approaches are conducted simultaneously. Most public institutions (which total 44) are granted a self-accrediting status, with the autonomy to develop review standards to accredit their own programs. They can be exempted from the audit of the Tertiary Education Quality and Standards Agency (TEQSA). However, more than 150 non-self-accrediting institutions are required to be reviewed by TEQSA within a seven-year cycle (TEQSA 2013a, b).

Like Australia, Hong Kong has also adopted the dual track system, but self-accrediting status is only granted to eight public institutions funded by the University Grants Committee (UGC). The self-accrediting institutions can accredit their own programs, but they still must be reviewed externally by two quality assurance agency bodies on a regular basis: the Quality Assurance Council (QAC) for degree programs and the Joint Quality Review Committee (JQRC) for sub-degree programs. Instead of granting institutions a specific status, such as being accredited, or denied, the two quality assurance agencies only give recommendation reports for the self-accrediting institutions (Wong 2013; UGC 2014; Cheng and Leung 2014). The other non-self-accrediting institutions are mostly private institutions that have to be accredited regularly by the Hong Kong Council for Accreditation of Academic and Vocational Qualifications (HKCAAVQ).

In 2008, Malaysia initiated a self-accrediting system and eight universities, including four public universities, and four international branch campuses were invited to apply for it. In 2010, the MOE announced that the eight universities were granted a self-accrediting status after Ministry of Education (MOA's) review (MQA 2014). Except for the eight universities, all other Higher Education Institutions (HEIs) are non-self-accrediting institutions which have to be reviewed every five years by the Malaysian Qualifications Agency (MQA) under "the Code of Practice for Institutional Audit (COPIA)" for institutional audit and "the Code of Practice for Program Accreditation (COPPA)" for program audit (MQA 2012). According to MQA, the self-accrediting institutions need to comply with the review standards in COPIA and COPPA. In addition, self-accreditation is only applied to general programs as professional programs are not included (e.g. programs in medicine or law) (MQA 2014). However, MQA will still consistently advise self-accrediting institutions regularly in order to ensure their quality.

Generally speaking, accreditation status in these four countries is approved by the governing MOE and usually given to public sector institutions with a well-established internal quality assurance mechanism. Concurrently, self-accrediting institutions are still required to comply with the standards and the criteria developed by national quality assurance agencies, being assessed by them on a regular basis.

Taiwan Policy

The MOE determined to launch its "self-accreditation" policy in 2012 in order to respond to various requests to increase university autonomy and to strengthen internal quality assurance activities (MOE 2013). Self-accrediting universities are expected to realize their strengths and weaknesses as well as to develop their own review standards. At the same time, they will be given authority to conduct an external evaluation over their programs without being reviewed by HEEACT. The new policy represents a dual quality assurance system in Taiwan higher education dividing institutions into "self-accrediting" and "non-self-accrediting" types.

According to the MOE, universities can apply for self-accreditation status if they meet one of the following requirements: (1) they are recipients of MOE grants of the Development Plan for World Class Universities and Research Centers of Excellence; (2) recipients of MOE grants of the Top University Project; and (3) recipients of MOE grants for the Teaching Excellence Project providing more than 6.7 million in USD over a consecutive four years. Currently, these are 34 institutions eligible for application.

Applicants for self-accrediting status engage a two-stage process. In the first stage, the applicant is required to submit documents and evidence demonstrating its capacity to conduct an internal review process. All documents will be reviewed by a recognition committee organized by the MOE. The review standards include eight aspects (MOE 2013):

1. The university has set up its own self-accreditation regulations based on the consensus of the whole university.
2. The self-accreditation standards developed by the university are properly integrated with its educational goals and uniqueness.
3. A steering committee of self-accreditation is organized by the university and its responsibility is properly defined in the regulations. The committee consists of three to five outside university experts.
4. The whole review process of the self-accreditation is properly designed with multiple data resources and a self-improvement function.
5. The peer reviewers should be comprised of experienced experts, academic scholars, and industry representatives.
6. The self-accreditation system is fully supported by the university itself with enough financial support and human resources.
7. A feedback system set up by the university continuously makes self-improvements according to the accreditation results and the review comments.

8. The self-accreditation results are transparent and will be announced to the public.

The second stage focuses on the actual review process and procedure conducted by self-accrediting institutions and recognizes review outcomes submitted by the self-accrediting institutions. The audit will be carried out by HEEACT through document checks. After going through and approving HEEACT's audit, the MOE will allow self-accrediting institutions to publish their review outcomes.

Given the fact that universities are given autonomy to develop their particular features through a self-accreditation process and related procedures, they will be able to determine if they would like to operate either internationally or remain local. The MOE does not set up specific regulations for either set of review criteria or the composition of a review panel, but many applicants tend to strengthen the "internationalization" character within the review procedures. One third of applicants incorporated an "internationalization" aspect into one of the review items, such as enhancing students' foreign language proficiency, deepening campus internationalization, developing faculty international capacities, and so on. Moreover, several research-oriented universities decided to invite international reviewers to join their on-site visit. Taiwan National University, for example, stipulated that all program reviews should include at least one international reviewer in the review panel. To conclude, Taiwan's self-accreditation system has three characteristics: first, universities are given autonomy to develop their own standards and external review system; second, self-accreditation is only applied for program level accreditation, not for institutional accreditation, for which HEEACT remains responsible; and third, the review process of self-accreditation status is divided into two stages conducted by the MOE and HEEACT, respectively (Hou et al. 2014).

Research Method and Subjects: The Case of Fu Jen Catholic University

Fu Jen was selected as a case study to document how MOE's self-accreditation policy impacts Taiwan higher education. The study conducted a survey targeting 55 reviewed programs and 267 reviewers for their input on the design and implementation of self-accreditation at Fu Jen. The total number of questionnaires distributed was 503 with an overall response rate of 72.23 percent. All respondents were asked to fill out

5-point scale questionnaires and to present their opinions regarding four categories and 23 questions, including their views on whether the self-accreditation was implemented successfully, whether it was having a positive impact on the aspects of the institution, including faculty engagement, the writing of the self-study report for on-site visits, and the overall impact on quality improvement. All questions are simply analyzed by mean and standard deviation (STD), and then, histograms and normal curves were employed as two checking tools to summarize how respondents' attitudes toward the questions were distributed on the 5-point scales.

Established in 1961, Fu Jen Catholic University was the first Catholic higher education institution in Taiwan. Affiliated with three religious orders, Fu Jen has emerged as a comprehensive doctoral-intensive university with an approximate enrollment of 26,000 and 710 full-time faculty members organized into 12 colleges, including Medicine, Management, Liberal Arts, Law, Art, Communication, Education, Foreign Languages, Social Sciences, Science and Engineering, Human Ecology, and the School of Continuing Education.

Fu Jen emphasizes a diversified, holistic, interdisciplinary, and international learning environment. Assisted by scientific research, Fu Jen has been committed to "the pursuit of truth and the integration of western and Chinese cultural values so as to promote the well-being of the human family and strengthen world solidarity". In the first cycle of program accreditation, 82 out of 86 programs of Fu Jen were accredited by HEEACT, yielding a pass rate of 95.3 percent. In 2011, Fu Jen was reaccredited by HEEACT institutional assessment with a 100 percent pass. In addition, Fu Jen is the only institution with three professional accreditations within Taiwan: the Association to Advance Collegiate Schools of Business (AACSB), the Institute of Engineering Education Taiwan (IEET), and the Taiwan Medical Accreditation Council (TMAC). In 2013, the MOE in Taiwan recognized Fu Jen as one of 34 self-accrediting institutions. By May 2014, a total of 55 programs had been reviewed completely through the self-accreditation process. MOE has finally approved the review outcomes in 2016.

Major Findings

In order to develop a self-accrediting review system, Fu Jen has passed the requirements of the Self-Accreditation Regulation as well as undergone several organizational reforms, including setting up a Center for Academic Development and Evaluation, organizing an Evaluation

Steering Committee, and establishing three tiers of Evaluation Executive Committees (at university, collegiate, and department levels). The following analyses present the attitudes of the reviewer and program heads, faculty members, and staff toward the self-accreditation implementation process and impacts at Fu Jen and suggest how they contribute toward creating a culture of quality.

Design and Mechanism

The first category asks the respondent whether the plan and design of self-accreditation, including review criteria, indicators, reviewer selection, review procedures, and an appeal system, are appropriate. Table 2.1 indicates that responses from reviewers agreed highly on all items from the covered programs. The items to which the reviewers gave the highest score were "Appeal system" and "Three review outcomes". University respondents, on the other hand, gave their highest agreement to the item "questions addressed by the reviewers one day before the on-site visits". They appeared to believe that this mechanism would assist them to clarify some questions in the self-study report addressed by the reviewers. When it came to the item on which the respondents agreed least, two were indicated: "Deletion of criteria and indicators" and "Organization

Table 2.1 Comparison among UK, Australia, Hong Kong, and Malaysia in self-accreditation

Item	UK	Australia	Hong Kong	Malaysia
Goal	Universities are given autonomy to award degree	Universities are given autonomy to award degree	Universities are given autonomy to award degree	Universities are given autonomy to award degree
Type of universities	Public university and further college	Public university	Public university	Research university and International Branch Campuses (IBCs)
Number	36	44	8	8
External review agency	By QAA	TEQSA	QAC/ JQRC	MQA
Review standards	IQA mechanism	IQA mechanism	Teaching and learning quality	IQA mechanism

Table 2.2 Respondents' attitude toward self-accreditation design and mechanism by reviewers and universities

Category	Reviewers (N=177)		Reviewed programs (N=137)	
	Mean	SD	Mean	SD
The review period and scope only cover the teaching and research activities in the previous three years	4.32	0.632	3.88	0.734
Deletion of criteria and indicators	4.22	0.660	3.89	0.759
Completion of self-study before self-accreditation	4.63	0.507	4.11	0.669
Questions prepared before the on-site	4.46	0.489	4.32	0.614
Reviewers' recommendation	4.43	0.600	4.23	0.723
Conflict of interest mechanism for reviewers	4.48	0.585	4.29	0.638
On-site procedures, including presentation, document check, interviews, etc.	4.56	0.498	4.17	0.609
Appeal system is needed	4.58	0.494	4.25	0.627
Three result outcomes: accredited, conditionally accredited, and denial	4.58	0.529	4.06	0.694
Organization and human resources of the program will be determined by review results	4.41	0.579	3.54	0.892

and human resources of the program will be determined by review results", respectively, by the reviewers and university-level respondents. It could be seen that reviewers were worried that some important criteria and indicators were deleted or revised by the reviewed program, which would likely lead to quality deterioration. In contrast, university respondents did not apparently think the review outcomes should be used for program closure or merger or even budget cuts (Table 2.2).

Understanding and Engagement

When respondents were asked if the stakeholders understood the purpose and importance of self-accreditation, the level of agreement by reviewers was much higher than that of university respondents. However, both agreed that students perceived them less than faculty and staff did. In addition, it could also be found that university respondents did not think they were assisted completely by the Center for Academic Development and Evaluation, which received a lowest score of 3.62. At the same time,

Table 2.3 Level of university stakeholders' understanding and engagement in the self-accreditation procedures by reviewer and universities

Category	Reviewers (N=176)		Reviewed programs (N=137)	
	Mean	SD	Mean	SD
Faculty members understand the purpose and importance of self-accreditation	4.68	0.504	4.25	0.071
Students understand the purpose and importance of self-accreditation	4.47	0.575	4.01	0.749
Staff understand the purpose and importance of self-accreditation	4.68	0.493	4.44	0.626
Quality office offers sufficient support to reviewed programs	–	–	3.62	0.893
Qualification of reviewers	–	–	4.01	0.759

they also did not think all reviewers were sufficiently qualified to review them (Table 2.3).

Self-Study Report Writing

Writing a self-study report is one of the biggest challenges for the reviewed program. A good report needs to integrate coverage of various parts of the program and present it as a coherent whole. It will "involve a process of self-reflection by the review units being reviewed and the preparation of a document reflecting that self-reflection" (INQAAHE 2013). The report not only contains information about the state of current program development but also points out the strengths and weaknesses that the reviewed program faces. According to the survey, reviewers were quite satisfied with the quality of the self-study report prepared by the reviewed program. The item they were most concerned with was that which inquired if the self-improvement plan had been presented clearly in the report, to which they provided a relatively low aggregate score of 4.14. As to the university respondents, they were considerably more worried about whether their self-study reports indeed demonstrated the current development, strengths, and weaknesses of their programs completely. In addition, they expected that they would be given sufficient time to write the self-study report (Table 2.4).

Table 2.4   Respondents' attitude toward quality of self-study report by reviewers and universities

Category	Reviewers (N=177)		Reviewed programs (N=137)	
	Mean	SD	Mean	SD
Current development of the reviewed programs can be described clearly in a set of indicators and criteria	4.36	0.537	3.74	0.783
Strengths and weaknesses can be presented clearly in a set of indicators and criteria	4.35	0.566	3.68	0.742
Self-study report can demonstrate the strengths of the reviewed program specifically	4.34	0.603	–	–
Self-study can point out the challenges that the reviewed program faces	4.25	0.637	–	–
Self-improvement plan is presented in the self-study report	4.14	0.724	–	–
Self-study report assists reviewers to assess the reviewed program	4.42	0.630	–	–
Reviewed program has sufficient time to complete the self-study report	–	–	3.81	0.721

On-site Visits

According to INQAAHE (2013), "On-site visits, which often last several days, are part of the quality evaluation process". A team of reviewers visits the reviewed institutions or programs to check on the veracity of the self-study report. At Fu Jen, an on-site visit lasts only one and a half days. In other words, the reviewers needed to scrutinize all related facilities and documents and conduct interviews with staff and students within one and a half days. The survey indicated that reviewers were less satisfied with the duration of the on-site visit. They did not agree that they had been provided enough time to assess the various programs in a satisfactory manner. The same response came from university respondents as well. However, reviewers highly agreed on the merit of the assistance from the Center of Academic Development and Evaluation. On the contrary, however, university respondents did not think they were supported well by the center (Table 2.5).

Table 2.5 Respondents' attitude toward on-site visits by reviewers and universities

Category	Reviewers (N=177)		Reviewed programs (N=137)	
	Mean	SD	Mean	SD
Reviewer have enough time to assess the program with one and a half days' on-site visit	4.11	0.879	4.19	0.762
Pre-review meeting assists the reviewers to communicate with each other before on-site visit	4.40	0.592	–	
Reviewed program can provide related and relevant documents on the day of on-site visit	4.33	0.634	–	
Reviewed program can provide related information or respond immediately when the reviewers address some questions	4.58	0.567	–	
Reviewers complete the review procedure according to the predefined schedule	–		4.24	0.783
Predefined schedule is followed by the reviewed program	4.67	0.483	4.47	0.593
Staff of QA Office are very helpful on the day of on-site visit	4.70	0.486	4.04	0.856

Self-Accreditation Impact

When it comes to the impact of self-accreditation, reviewers highly agreed that the whole system and procedures indeed assisted the reviewed programs to improve their quality. In contrast, university respondents tended to be more conservative about the actual impact of the process on overall program quality improvement (Table 2.6).

DISCUSSION AND CONCLUSION

Striking a balance between autonomy and quality is still a challenging process. The purpose of self-accreditation is to give institutions more autonomy to develop their individual features and strengthen internal quality assurance mechanisms. The Fu Jen study demonstrated that this objective has not yet been achieved. The new policy emphasized that self-accrediting universities have been given autonomy to decide review criteria and indicators, which indeed had worried most reviewers. It was also found that some institutions deleted several important indicators in order

Table 2.6 Respondents' attitude toward the impact on reviewed program by reviewers and universities

Category	Reviewers (N=177)		Reviewed programs (N=137)	
	Mean	SD	Mean	SD
Final report assists the reviewed program how to improve themselves	4.53	0.534	3.88	0.704
Self-accreditation improves establishment of internal quality assurance and university quality	4.56	0.544	3.75	0.802

to avoid being assessed by them (Chen and Hou 2015). These practices indeed influence the quality of universities themselves as well as damage the core value of the MOE self-accreditation policy.

The attitude of reviewers toward self-accreditation tended to be positive in comparison with that of university respondents. The self-accreditation policy seems to be better recognized and given more value by reviewers than by universities, including the elements of the plan, self-study report, on-site visit, and impact. Self-accreditation aims at liberating universities from the national accreditor, HEEACT, but it is not as yet highly recognized as such by universities. At the campus level, it even remains difficult for universities to engage their own faculty and students in the process of self-accreditation

A well-supported QA office is a high expectation for reviewed programs to possess. In order to implement self-accreditation, universities need to set up a QA office with sufficient resources and experienced personnel to properly undergo a review. However, in practice, most programs undergoing review appear to believe that the support from the QA office should be enhanced and that the role of the QA office should be strengthened. Therefore, how to build the capacity of the QA office appears to be a subject that requires urgent attention in order for this overall program of self-accreditation to be sustained.

A gap continues to exist between reviewers and universities in terms of the impact of self-accreditation on university quality improvement. The survey shows that universities and reviewers have different attitudes toward the relative effectiveness and impacts of the process. The finding that reviewers tend to be more positive than university respondents about the process indicates that it will take universities a longer time to achieve the objective of achieving a quality culture building within campuses.

In conclusion, we can see that self-accreditation has already been implemented in several Asian countries, including Taiwan. As a latecomer to these practices, the Taiwan government is attempting to build universities' capacities by giving them more autonomy. However, it remains a very challenging job for universities to strike a balance between the often-perceived conflict between accountability and autonomy. From the perspective of universities, self-accreditation will definitely encourage them to develop their distinct features and strengths through a well-established internal quality assurance mechanism. In reality and perhaps in future practice, some important review items will likely be deleted or neglected by reviewed programs or units given that they lack support and their perception of utility.

The Fu Jen case demonstrates that reviewers tend to be more positive about the self-accreditation system than the university faculty and staff themselves. When it comes to the perceived effectiveness of self-accreditation, the gap is even bigger. It seems that university respondents have a more conservative attitude toward self-accreditation's potential and actual impacts on higher education. The result seems to indicate that it will likely take universities a greater period of time to develop their quality culture in a manner that is firmly rooted on campus.

REFERENCES

Chen, K., & Hou, A. Y. C. (2015). *The newly launched self-accreditation system in Taiwan and its impact on internal quality assurance of institutions.* Presented at 2015 INQAAHE conference, Chicago.

Cheng, M. A., & Leung, N. W. (2014). Quality assurance of non-local accounting programs conducted in Hong Kong. *Higher Education Studies, 4*(5), 47–61.

Harvey, L. (2014). Analytic quality glossary, quality research international. http://www.qualityresearchinternational.com/glossary/. Accessed 15 Jan 2015.

Higher Education Evaluation & Accreditation Council of Taiwan (HEEACT). (2011). *Handbook of institutional accreditation.* Taipei: HEEACT.

Higher Education Evaluation & Accreditation Council of Taiwan (HEEACT). (2012). *2011 annual report.* Taipei: HEEACT.

Higher Education Evaluation & Accreditation Council of Taiwan (HEEACT). (2014). *2013 annual report.* Taipei: HEEACT.

Higher Education Evalualtion & Accreditation Council of Taiwan (HEEACT) (2016). HEEACT website. http://www.heeact.edu.tw/sp.asp?xdurl=appraise/appraise_list.asp&ctNode=491&mp=2

Hou, A. Y. C. (2011). Quality assurance at a distance: International accreditation in Taiwan higher education. *Higher Education, 61*(2), 179–191.

Hou, A. Y. C., Chen, K., & Morse, R. (2014). Transforming the quality assurance framework for Taiwanese higher education: A glonacal context. *Policy and Society, 33*, 275–285.

International Network for Quality Assurance Agencies in Higher Education (INQAAHE) (2013). Analytic quality glossary. Retrieved December 1, 2013, from http://www.qualityresearchinternational.com/glossary/selfaccreditation.htm

Kinser, K. (2011). Multinational quality assurance. *New Directions for Higher Educations, 155*, 53–64.

Malaysia Qualifications Agency (MQA) (2012). 2011 annual report. http://www.mqa.gov.my/portal2012/publications/reports/annual/Laporan%20Tahunan%202011.pdf. Accessed 22 Dec 2014.

Malaysia Qualification Agency (MQA). (2014). Self-accreditation. http://www.mqa.gov.my/. Accessed on 25 Feb 2014.

Ministry of Education (MOE). (2013). *Provisions of self–accrediting institutions' atatus recognitions and review outcomes' approval.* Taipei: Ministry of Education.

Sanyal, B. C., & Martin, M. (2007). Quality assurance and the role of accreditation: An overview. In Global University Network for Innovation (Ed.), *Higher education in the world 2007: Accreditation for quality assurance: What is at stake?* (pp. 3–17). New York: Palgrave Macmillan.

Stensaker, B., Langfeldt, L., Harvey, L., Huisman, J., & Westerheijden, D. (2011). An in-depth study on the impact of external quality assurance. *Assessment & Evaluation in Higher Education, 36*(4), 465–478.

Tertiary Education Quality and Standards Agency (TEQSA). (2013a). TEQSA annual report 2012–13. http://www.teqsa.gov.au/news-publications/annual-reports/2013. Accessed 22 Feb 2014.

Tertiary Education Quality and Standards Agency (TEQSA). (2013b). Self-accrediting authority. http://www.teqsa.gov.au/for-providers. Accessed 20 Dec 2014.

University Grants Committee (UGC). (2014). Quality assurance of UGC. http://www.ugc.edu.hk/eng/ugc/activity/qa/quality.htm. Accessed 1 Mar 2015.

Wong, W. S. (2013). *External quality assurance under a self-accreditation system: Promoting and assessing internal quality assurance.* Paper presented at the 2013 Conference of International Network for Quality Assurance Agencies in Higher Education (INQAAHE), April 8–11, Taiwan.

CHAPTER 3

From Strategic Thinking to a Plan of Action: The Process of Mapping Organizational Quality: A Case Study of the USC Rossier School of Education

Cathryn L. Dhanatya

Introduction

What is strategic planning? The idea of allowing organizations to "think" and "contemplate" their future enterprises through some disciplined process is not a new phenomenon. The process of strategic planning can be seen everywhere, from complex large-scale multinational corporations and government to small-scale businesses and non-profits. This focus on planning has allowed organizations of all sizes to engage in process in which actors think, strategize, develop, and implement measureable strategies and outcomes that define both internal and external success and quality. According to Steiner, the definition of strategic planning can be elaborated into four main points of view:

C.L. Dhanatya (✉)
Williams Institute, UCLA School of Law,
Los Angeles, CA, USA

© The Author(s) 2017
D.E. Neubauer, C. Gomes (eds.),
Quality Assurance in Asia-Pacific Universities,
DOI 10.1007/978-3-319-46109-0_3

(1) strategic planning deals with the futurity of current decisions allowing managers to reflect, plan, and think of solutions or change course based on data that is presented; (2) strategic planning is a process that allows managers to set organizational aims, goals and develop strategies to implement those goals in a timely and iterative manner; (3) strategic planning is an attitude, a philosophy and a way of life; it is the ability for the managers to intellectualize and contemplate the future of their organization and envision the possibilities based on current resources and data to plan for the future in a concrete manner; and finally (4) strategic planning is a formal structure that links three main types of plans: strategic plans, medium range programs, and short term budgets and operating plans allowing for the ability of the organization to have broad understanding of how it is developing and changing various time horizons. (2008)

The history of strategic planning is seen as early as 1965 in the literature related to management studies. From the 1950s, strategic planning was mainly an exercise in the budgeting process, but by the mid-1960s, it had become an entrenched part of corporate American culture and government in the form of the planning, programming, and budgeting systems (Mintzberg 1994; Gilmore 1970; and Chamberlain 1968). However, the concept of strategic planning as a means to think and reflect and forecast what an enterprise should be doing in the following years or decades to come has literary origins as early as Sun Tzu's treatise *Art of War* written over 2 millennia ago (1971; Mintzberg 1994). At its basic level, strategic planning allows for organizations regardless of size to develop a shared vision, create strategies, and set medium- and long-term goals for growth and development. Generally, strategic plans are comprised of three main elements: the (1) vision or mission statement that sets aspirational goals for the organization; (2) listing of proposed initiatives that the organization will engage in to promote those aspirational goals and (3) budgeting for the initiatives (Martin 2014).

However, while many organizations are engaging in some form of strategic planning and, at times, providing significant financial and human capital toward such endeavors, according to *Harvard Business Review,* "95% of a company's employees are unaware of, or do not understand, its strategy. If the employees who are closest to customers and who operate processes that create value are unaware of the strategy, then they surely cannot help the organization implement it effectively" (Kaplan and Norton, 2005). This issue of internal communications becomes a key barrier to the successful execution of a strategic planning process. If all stakeholders are not on the same page, then there tends to be confusion and an inability to effectively execute the goals and strategies developed through the planning process. Therefore, the development of plans from the strategic planning process must have a level of clarity, coherence and simplicity in order to engage a diversity of stakeholders to implement and understand the planning process and the subsequent work product developed.

When done correctly, strategic planning can be a powerful tool to develop internal coherence and organizational movement toward a singular set of goals. Through this comprehensive process, there is a requirement for an organization to internally assess and reflect upon how each organization defines success which also relates to conversations of the development of quality products and services. In the majority of US higher education research institutions, the mission of these institutions is to produce high-quality research, effective teaching and preparation of an educated workforce, and service to the greater community. In order to service these charges, institutions of higher education have adopted strategic planning as a means to develop and articulate goals, strategies and definitions of institutional success over the long term.

Although historically the process of strategic planning began as a means for corporate and business leaders to assess their organization's current state and articulate and align goals and strategies for growth and development over a period of three to five years, this process has now been widely adopted by all different types of institutions, including those in US higher education. Strategic planning has become an integral part of the accreditation process in which strategic plan documents are often reviewed as part of the site visit documents. The accreditation process is "used in US education to ensure that schools, postsecondary institutions, and other education providers meet, and maintain, minimum standards of quality and integrity regarding academics, administration, and related services" (US Department of Education Website, 2008). Accredited programs are seen to have a "stamp" of approval in terms of achieving a certain standard of quality, marker of rigor, and legitimacy providing the accredited institution with better access to governmental funding in the form of student aid and research funding. Accredited programs in turn are more likely to attract high-caliber faculty and students to teach and attend the institution. They are also more likely to be viewed and considered favorably by prospective employers of graduates from those programs. The US accreditation process also allows for the massification and standardization of markers of quality in which top-tier institutions of higher education are ranked, and the public opinion of their quality becomes more reliant on what Gavin explains as "perceived quality" (1988) or rather reputation and brand recognition than empirical data. The issue with accreditation, as Lindborg and Spangehl argue, is that the general public only "vaguely" understands what the term actually historically and contextually encompasses and that the overall "quality" can still vary greatly among accredited institutions (2011). Nonetheless, accreditation still is a key indicator that dictates legitimacy and quality among educational institutions in the USA. Therefore, university and school strategic plans have become integral parts of the document review process and are meant to articulate and illustrate the goals, visions and progress the university and its relevant departments are striving for to successfully implement their mission.

This chapter discusses a case study of the strategic planning process for the University of Southern California (USC) Barbara and Roger Rossier School of Education beginning in 2011 and culminated in the 2012–2015 Strategic Plan for the Rossier School of Education. The case study will outline the planning process, consensus building, the final outcomes, and subsequent adoption of a continuous improvement and development model for refining the strategic plan on an ongoing basis.

The case study is located within the USC's Rossier School of Education. USC is one of US's premier research institutions. The University has garnered international prestige and respect for its academic programming, research, community engagement, the high caliber of its faculty and students, and world-class facilities, including multiple libraries, laboratories and classrooms. The university raised over $687 million in research funding in the fiscal year 2014–15 and has an operating budget of approximately $3.9 billion annually with a $4.6 billion endowment (USC Facts and Figures Website, 2015). According to the 2014 US News and World Report, USC currently ranks 23rd among all US universities and currently serves about 43,000 students (19,000 undergraduates and 24,000 graduate students) (USC Facts and Figures Website, 2015). For the past century, USC's Rossier School of Education has developed and prepared professional leaders in the field of education and research, including teachers, superintendents, administrative professionals, policy leaders and scholars.

Renowned for its groundbreaking use of technology in teaching, USC Rossier has been on the forefront of innovation in creating the Master's of Arts in Teaching (MAT@USC) online degree program in partnership with a corporate partner, 2U, Inc. The MAT@USC, the first online teacher education preparation program offered by a tier-one research institution, has received numerous awards for innovation and best practices, including the American Council of Education's 2011 International Award for Innovative Practices and the American Association of Colleges of Teacher Education 2010 Best Practices Award for Innovative Use of Technology. As of February 2011, more than 1500 students are enrolled in the MAT@ USC program from 45 US states and 25 foreign countries, including Turkey, Japan and South Korea.

The four thriving research centers at Rossier are the epitome of the synergy between academic research theory and praxis. The Center on Educational Governance (CEG), the Pullias Center for Higher Education, the Center for Urban Education (CUE), and the Center for Enrollment Research, Policy and Practice (CERPP) are leading the field in studying effective and non-effective strategies for high-need student populations with a special focus on urban low-income students of color. The work of the centers looks to directly improve outcomes for learners at all levels.

The strength of USC Rossier's international reputation is based on the application of research, not simply its theoretical construct. Research-based tools, developed in conjunction with educational practitioners, are now being utilized in schools and universities across the country. The success and the growing market for these evidence-based education products are a testament to the USC Rossier School's commitment to producing relevant research that makes a difference. USC Rossier has also had a long track record of recruiting individual schools and school districts to participate in research studies. Faculty members from Rossier have conducted numerous research studies of schools in Los Angeles Unified School District (LAUSD) and in a variety of states, ranging from California, Ohio, Florida to Louisiana. One of the key partnerships to highlight this work is a partnership with LAUSD and a team of USC Rossier faculty who were awarded the prestigious US Department of Education Investing in Innovation (i3) Development grant for a study on the LAUSD Public School Choice Initiative.

The research developed by USC Rossier's faculty has also impacted critical legislation through its leadership organizations such as PACE (Policy Analysis for California Education). Along with colleagues from Stanford and UC-Davis, USC faculty are actively engaged with state policymakers to enrich education policy debates through sound research analysis and hard evidence. USC Rossier's faculty are noteworthy for their multiple appointments, awards, federal grants, national board of leadership and international partnerships. They have published hundreds of books and articles and served as editors of the most prestigious journals in the field, as officers of all the leading professional associations, and as members of significant international and federal panels on critical education issues. The overall qualities of the school, its faculty and work product have combined over time to create a demonstrable culture of quality through which the activities of the school flow.

STRATEGIC THINKING WEEK

The USC Rossier School has been led by Emory Stoops and Joyce King Stoops Dean Karen Symms Gallagher since 2000. In her tenure, Dean Gallagher has implemented the groundbreaking, award winning fully online MAT Program, has launched two university-affiliated charter high schools in high-need areas within the Los Angeles Unified School District, and has raised the rankings of the USC Rossier School to 21 according to the *U.S. News and World Report*. Dean Gallagher is often quoted saying "The Rossier School of Education is not your grandmother's School of Education." What she means by this is that Rossier School strives to achieve its mission of "improving urban education locally, nationally, and globally." Through her vision and ability to mobilize the various units throughout the school, Dean Gallagher developed, along with her senior leadership team, the idea for Strategic Thinking Week in the summer of 2011 in order to plan and develop ideas for the upcoming Rossier Strategic Plan.

Strategic Thinking Week was a mandated convening of identified key stakeholder groups to meet and discuss the possibilities and goals for the next five years. (USC Rossier Strategic Planning Process, 2011). These groups included high-level Rossier administrators, faculty, and staff, as well as senior administrators from other comparable higher education institutions and outside supporters. "The Strategic Thinking Week" was then facilitated by two outside management and training consultants and a meeting capture artist, whose responsibility is to synthesize meeting discussions into a pictorial form in real time. The convening consisted of a series of large group meetings and smaller work groups to discuss and reflect upon current practices and policies and make considered decisions about which of these policies should be kept, developed, modified or abandoned for the future.

The opening exercise had all of the stakeholders present to discuss and contemplate the current vision and mission of the school. Stakeholders came to a consensus as a group about the key drivers and outcomes for the school. Framing this process, the mission of the Rossier School was to "strengthen urban education locally, nationally, and globally." The outcomes of this initial discussion can be seen in Fig. 3.1.

Figure 3.1 illustrates on the left side the inputs or drivers that would attract students and faculty to the Rossier School (i.e. quality of academic and professional development programs, quality and caliber of research and scholarship by the Rossier faculty and the relationships built within the field of education and greater education community). The second area is the interaction of the four academic concentrations (i.e. K-12 Leadership and Policy, Education Psychology, Teaching in Multicultural Societies, or TEMS, and Higher Education) within the school and suggests that they work collaboratively and individually to produce high-quality research and academic programs within an urban education context. The immediate desired outcomes are represented on the right side, which include graduating high-quality education leaders, producing high-quality and impactful research publications, addressing policies that improve urban education, and developing mutually beneficial partnerships with the community and key stakeholders within the field of education. The ultimate articulated outcome was that by 2020 the USC Rossier School of Education would be considered by the field of education to be an undisputedly impactful school of education. Initially, what developed out of this exercise was the ability to collectively reflect on current assets the Rossier School possessed and how to leverage those assets into outcomes that were meaningful and important to the collective group.

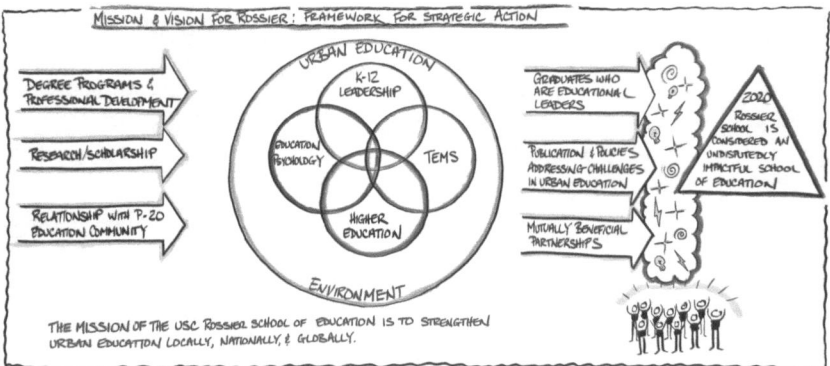

Fig. 3.1 Outcomes of mission and vision for Rossier discussion

The next sets of group activities were related to themes of satisfaction and individual care and importance. The larger group of participants was broken down into smaller groups that were charged with brainstorming and discussing the following prompt: "What gives you the greatest satisfaction in working at Rossier?" Each group then discussed and developed its ideas of what were the driving forces that made working at Rossier worthwhile for the individual and what motivated people to stay. As illustrated in Fig. 3.2, the answers were both larger scale and particularly based on job function.

The key themes that emerged from the discussions were: (1) working for an organization that was striving to be disruptive of the status quo and embracing innovation and change; (2) meaningful collaboration and relationships at all levels, from research to teaching to colleagues; (3) being able to engage in student development academically and professionally; (4) engaging in meaningful and impactful work that is changing urban education for the better; (5) being part of a growing organization that supports diversity in its students and faculty; and (6) being part of an organization that is developing the education leaders of tomorrow. By providing a space for discussion about job satisfaction, the facilitators allowed the collective group to reflect in a positive way about where each individual is in respect to their current careers and the context of why they came to work for the Rossier School, but also more importantly, how the institu-

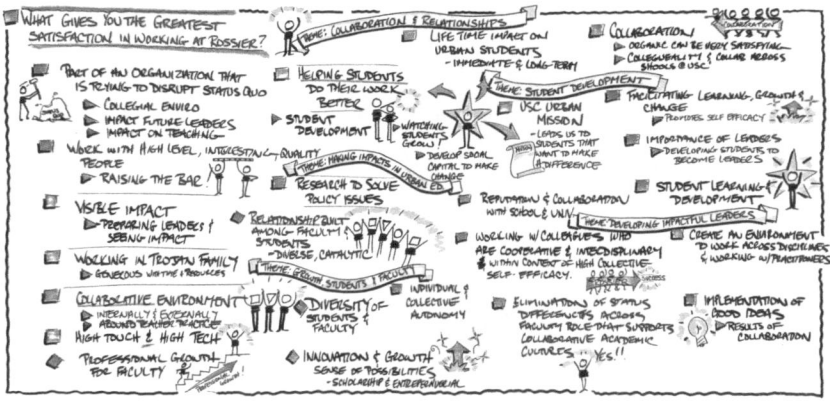

Fig. 3.2   Rossier work satisfaction map

tion is supporting that career development. This activity aimed to create a positive climate for discussion as it relates to the future of the school.

Following this exercise, within the smaller groups, participants were asked to reflect on what they care for the most about in urban education. Figure 3.3 shows the outcomes of those discussions.

The outcomes for this activity provided a strong grounding for the issues that mattered to groups when it came to impacting urban education. Through the exercise, individuals and the smaller groups were able to artic-

Fig. 3.3   Outcomes

ulate problems and aspirations that need to be examined and addressed if the Rossier School were to be an impactful school of education.

Following this focused collective activity, the next few days of Strategic Thinking Week would be spent in breakout groups organized by academic concentration. The goals of these facilitated, day-long sessions were that each academic concentration would meet and develop items organized around four areas: (1) environmental trends impacting the Rossier School, (2) distinguishing factors of the Rossier School, (3) future possibilities and (4) opportunities. After the four days of concentration meetings, the findings would be brought to the larger group through two-day integration meetings that would synthesize what was discussed, and then develop an integrated and cohesive articulation of assets, opportunities and bold ideas to pursue.

The final process of integration allowed for the group to collectively develop a coherent and shared mission, vision, value system and vocabulary for the Rossier School in regard to planning for the future. This mandated commitment of time was meant to engage stakeholders to feel that their opinions were valued and considered in the creation of the strategic plan over the next several months. This week-long convening would be the first step in incorporating stakeholder buy-in for the entire strategic planning and writing process.

USC ROSSIER 2012–2015 STRATEGIC PLAN WRITING PROCESS

The culmination of Strategic Thinking Week was a charge to a select committee to write the new Rossier Strategic Plan for 2012–2017. The committee was comprised of the Associate Dean for Research and Faculty Affairs, the Associate Dean for Academic Programs, the Chair of Faculty Council, two faculty members that were part of the Strategic Thinking Week planning committee and three Assistant Deans from Advancement, Research, and Communications, respectively. Over the next several months, building on the conversations and discussions from Strategic Thinking Week, the committee developed drafts of the strategic plan that incorporated the ideas and spirit of the conversations with additional refinements. These drafts were then subsequently reviewed by the faculty and staff to obtain feedback to be incorporated into the final plan that would be reviewed and approved by the Dean and the University Provost's office.

The outcomes from these drafts can be highlighted by the following key developments for the Rossier Strategic Plan. These were:

- A revision of the mission statement and creation of a vision statement
- Development of guiding values and distinctive characteristics
- Building on the current Rossier academic pillars (leadership, accountability, diversity, and learning)
- The importance of aligned goals, strategies, and implementation plans that can be monitored
- The importance of alignment to the greater university's strategic plan

The final strategic plan was developed based on numerous conversations and ongoing dialogues between the writing committee and the Rossier faculty and staff. The writing process became an iterative refinement of drafts based on incorporating and addressing input and critique from the Rossier faculty and staff.

DEVELOPING THE STRATEGIC PLAN AS AN ITERATIVE PROCESS

Based on the conversations during Strategic Thinking Week and the subsequent meetings that occurred within the Strategic Plan Writing Group, it became clear to the committee that the previous mission statement for the USC Rossier School needed to be revised. The previous mission statement read: "to strengthen urban education locally, nationally and globally." However, the committee felt that the ideas of the stakeholders regarding their goals and work with the USC Rossier School should be impactful and better capture the idea of promoting positive change. The new USC Rossier Mission became to "**improve learning** in urban education locally, nationally and globally" ("USC Rossier Strategic Plan 2012–2017," 2012). This two-word addition of "improve learning" was significant. The committee argued that it provided a much stronger commitment of the USC Rossier School to impact positive change in a broad but specific way by improving learning in all forms whether formal, informal, or ongoing. The other major change to the mission was the definition for the term "urban education." Also, the USC Rossier School would undertake to define what improving learning and transforming urban education meant. These definitions, additions and clarifications were incorporated based on faculty and staff comments of an early draft of the strategic plan:

Urban education takes place within many contexts including pre-kindergarten through high school, in human services, higher education, and workplace settings. Urban areas typically have unique strengths including racial, ethnic, linguistic, and cultural diversity. Urban areas often face challenges associated with equity and access, poverty, density, mobility and immigration, environmental degradation and strained social conditions around housing, healthcare and crime. Our emphasis on and learning in urban contexts guides us as we generate knowledge that is applicable to contexts beyond the urban core.

We will transform urban education by:

- Leading the search for innovative, efficacious, and just solutions by engaging in collaborative translational research.
- Preparing and developing educational leaders who are change agents committed to urban education and who possess the competencies needed to address complex educational and social issues.
- Creating mutually beneficial partnerships to ensure our work is field-based and incorporates a diversity of perspectives and experiences. (USC Rossier Strategic Plan 2012–2017, 2012)

The faculty and staff also opined that missing from the previous five-year plan was a vision for the USC Rossier School, including an aspirational goal. With this in mind, the committee drafted and refined a new Vision Statement. However, the dominant premise was that it should be built on defined foundational and guiding values with distinctive characteristics:

Our vision is a world where every student, regardless of personal circumstance, is able to learn and succeed. We believe that USC Rossier, as a top tier research institution, has the responsibility and the ability to train the education leaders and to develop the innovative practices inclusive of equity and access that will help realize this vision. (USC Rossier Strategic Plan 2012–2017, 2012)

As illustrated by the revision of the Mission Statement and the creation of the new Vision Statement, the importance of incorporating feedback from faculty and staff was imperative in developing consensus and buy-in for the final approved plan. However, after an additional round of edits, it became clear that a need existed to discuss not just how the USC Rossier School would engage in its work, but what the values that define and inform that work would be. What values as a school of education are required to improve learning in urban education? Through these discussions with faculty and staff, the writing committee developed a Guiding Values Section. This section was built on the USC Rossier's core academic pillars, which had been adopted in the previous Strategic Plan of **"Leadership, Accountability, Diversity and Learning."** The guiding values are **"Results Oriented, Collaborative Inquiry, Combining Research and Practice, Innovation and Commitment to Diversity"** (USC Rossier Strategic Plan 2012–2017, 2012). These values would go on now to define and inform the work of the USC Rossier School at all levels.

In order to also build on what was discussed in Strategic Thinking Week and to align that with the University-wide Strategic Plan, the committee proposed that a section be developed to show how the USC Rossier School of Education was distinctive. This addition would help build on the discussions related to the characteristics that make USC Rossier unique and how the work of USC Rossier's faculty and staff are translational and transformative. The importance of alignment to the greater University-wide Strategic Plan was imperative because the USC Rossier plan would ultimately need to be approved by the University Provost in order to be implemented. Such alignment is required if only because the Rossier School is part of a larger institution and enterprise, and perforce, the goals for the school need to reflect the larger vision of the university and provide coherence. Absent this would create a situation of mixed messages related to the work of the university as a whole.

Taking account of the experiences of the collective group, the committee originally proposed the four distinctive characteristics of **scale, speed and agility, risk, and impact**. These were meant to highlight the Rossier School's focus on addressing issues within urban education with flexibility, speed, high impact and at a large scale. However, through feedback with faculty, ultimately an additional characteristic was added: **"integrity."** The telling argument was made that although it would be important to have large-scale change and impact in the work, if there was not integrity to these endeavors (a word that encapsulates honesty, compassion, and accountability), the overall enterprise would be meaningless. The faculty felt strongly that some combination of accountability and heart be mutually present. As illustrated in the development of this particular section, the writing process was a cooperative, collaborative and iterative process that engaged multiple stakeholders, and which ensured it did not just appear as a directive from the committee or the Dean.

The final section of the strategic plan was the development of three key goals and subsequent strategies and implementation plans for their achievement. The three goals are:

GOAL 1: To produce the highest quality translational urban education research. We will take an entrepreneurial approach that leverages technology to engage in research that reflects a scientific industry model of "Research and Development." Our research will be driven by the mission of our school and reflect the five characteristics that inform our work.

GOAL 2: 100 percent of Rossier graduates will enter their profession fully prepared and able to improve learning in urban education—through their research, ability to leverage technology, program or curriculum development, teaching, policy development or counseling, and intervention.

GOAL 3: Identify, create and maintain partnerships that are sustained, deliberate and strategically integrated with our degree programs and research efforts (USC Rossier School of Education Strategic Plan 2012–2017, 2012).

These goals are purposefully aligned with the USC Rossier School's Mission. The document included strategies to accomplish these goals and individual implementation plans with attached timelines and time frames in the appendices of the strategic plan, providing for greater accountability, monitoring and evaluation of the progress of these goals. By including strategies and implementation plans with timelines, the writing committee wanted to reinforce the idea and process of continuous dialogue and discussion. The purpose was to allow for the school to continue to monitor progress, but embrace the fact that the strategic plan ultimately was not static and would need to be revised as the context changed within the school over time. By allowing space for continued discussion and evaluation, the goal would be to promote a culture of continuous improvement and accountability (which is an element that appears to have some ubiquity within most higher education quality endeavors).

Since the approval of the USC Rossier School of Education Strategic Plan 2012–2017 by both the Dean and the Provost's Office, its goals and implementation have continued to develop and change. Each year, Dean Gallagher has created departmental charge documents for each area of the school based on the implementation of the strategic plan. These documents act as measurable guides for each subject area to develop their annual departmental goals in line with the mission, vision and goals. Changes have also been made to the implementation plan activities based on a refocusing of priorities or financial constraints that have arisen in the past three years since the plan was approved. However, what needs to be emphasized is that these changes and revisions have been agreed upon by the Rossier School of Education's Dean and the senior leadership team in consultation with various stakeholders, namely, faculty and staff. Yet the ultimate goal remains the same, which is to create and sustain the ability for the school to continue to engage in high-quality, meaningful and impactful work that will improve and transform education for those that have the highest need.

Conclusion

This case study examines how one US School of Education at a top-tier research institution engaged in a comprehensive exercise in strategic planning and how it has subsequently developed or changed the plan since its implementation in 2012. The intent has been to demonstrate how, at a very practical level, the school has sought to define, process and implement activities that will continue the culture of quality, which is held to be a harbinger of the school. Rossier was able to accomplish a vehicle that allows the various stakeholders in the organization to come together with coherence and intention to develop measurable goals and define success as a collective. The lessons that have been learned through this process include the importance of consensus building and buy-in from various stakeholders and remaining open and responsive to feedback. By creating space and time for the collective to think, write, react, and revise, the USC Rossier School leadership allowed stakeholders to feel that they were engaged and truly a part of the process in developing their organizational strategic plan for the next five years. This made for greater coherence in messaging, description of the ultimately approved strategic plan by stakeholders to the outside world, and the ability to have a shared responsibility and accountability for the strategic plan's implementation. The planning process also allowed for the development of shared identity and common language around success and quality for the school faculty and staff, which is a key indicator of success for highly functioning organizations.

Reflecting on this process, a few critiques have emerged. The first is that the USC Rossier School seemed to really work hard to incorporate feedback and buy-in for the process. However, a key constituency was missing, namely that students enrolled in the academic programs at the USC Rossier School were not included in the process. Given that the school must rely on tuition from these students to operate, it seems that not including their representation and input on the identification and statement of goals was problematic. If the school is unable to fully understand the needs of the population(s) it directly services, then there is a fundamental flaw in the process. Recognizing this, the writing committee recommended that in the next round of strategic planning student participation should be assured to enhance the collective understanding and experiences necessary to inform the appropriate development of goals and strategies.

The second critique concerns the replicability of the process for other organizations. A main driver of this work was the mandate of the Dean for her faculty and staff to engage in the process. She was able to mandate that schedules be cleared and that it be an organizational priority that all faculty and staff needed to participate in irrespective of desire or predisposition. In the majority of contexts for other organizations, this paradigm simply would not work. Although there is great value in being able to collectively contemplate and discuss how an organization defines quality or success and is able to develop strategies to meet goals, this is not always possible. For larger organizational components, other constraints arise with governance structure, institutional barriers, financial considerations, time and space limitations that would impinge on the effectiveness of this model.

However, what is possible is that managers and administrators can be open to ideas of promoting feedback and communication from their collective stakeholders. An old adage holds that "two brains are better than one." By engaging in meaningful and thoughtful conversations, managers at all levels can learn a great deal from their colleagues and their subordinates. No one individual can understand the complexity of every minute aspect of an organization of any significant size; therefore, feedback provides a greater ability to continue to build consensus, buy-in, coherence, job satisfaction and ultimately quality within the organization.

References

Chamberlain, N. W. (1968). *Enterprise and environment*. New York: McGraw-Hill.

Garvin, D. A. (1988). *Managing quality: The strategic and competitive edge*. New York: The Free Press.

Gilmore, F. F. (1970). *Formulation and advocacy of business policy*. Ithaca: Cornell University Press.

Kaplan, R., & Norton, D. (2005, October). The office of strategy management. *Harvard Business Review*. Retrieved September 15, 2015, from https://hbr.org/2005/10/the-office-of-strategy-management.

Lindborg, H., & Spangehl, S. D. (2011). U.S. higher education accreditation: A quality perspective. *ASQ Higher Education Brief, 4*(6). Available at: http://rube.asq.org/edu/us-higher-education-and-accreditation-a-quality-perspective.pdf. Accessed 31 Dec 2016.

Martin, R. (2014, January–February). The big lie of strategic planning. *Harvard Business Review*. Retrieved September 15, 2015, from https://hbr.org/2014/01/the-big-lie-of-strategic-planning.

Mintzberg, H. (1994). *The rise and fall of strategic planning: Reconceiving roles for planning, plans, planners.* New York: The Free Press.

Steiner, G. A. (2008). *Strategic planning: What every manager must know.* New York: Simon & Shuster Inc.

Sun Tzu. (1971). *The art of war.* New York: Oxford University Press.

USC Rossier Strategic Planning Process. (2011, August 1). Retrieved September 30, 2015, from http://rossier.usc.edu/staff-resources/strategic-thinking/strategic-thinking-week/

USC Rossier School of Education Strategic Plan 2012–2017. Website (2012, May 30). Retrieved August 1, 2015, from http://rossier.usc.edu/files/2008/08/USC-Rossier-Strategic-Plan1.pdf

US Department of Education Website. (2008). Retrieved May 31, 2016, from http://www2.ed.gov/about/offices/list/ous/international/usnei/us/edlite-accreditation.html

Assuring Quality in Transnational Higher Education: A Case Study of Sino-Foreign Cooperation University in China

Han Xiao and Xiaojun Zhang

INTRODUCTION

Transnational higher education (TNHE) is widely understood as "all types of higher education study where the learners are located in a country different from the one where the awarding institution is based" (UNESCO/ Council of Europe 2001). It appears as many forms, such as branch campuses, franchises, articulation, twinning, corporate programs, online learning and distance education programs, and study abroad (Global Alliance for Transnational Education 1999). Some researchers have also adopted other terms such as cross-border education, offshore education, or borderless education to describe the real or virtual movement of students, faculty, and education programs from one country to another. Even while there may be some conceptual differences, these terms are often used interchangeably. However, borderless education neglects the existence of borders, which play a key role in regulatory work and quality assur-

H. Xiao (✉) • X. Zhang
Asian and Policy Studies, The Education University of Hong Kong,
Hong Kong, China

© The Author(s) 2017
D.E. Neubauer, C. Gomes (eds.),
Quality Assurance in Asia-Pacific Universities,
DOI 10.1007/978-3-319-46109-0_4

ance analyses (Knight 2006). According to Chinese regulations, the term TNHE denotes all the equivalent terms adopted by individual countries except the ones that ignore the existence of borders such as "borderless education". Specifically, this study focuses on the degree-conferring cooperative activities of or beyond undergraduate education.

Ever since the early 1990s, a wide variety of cross-border programs and providers have emerged, enabling students to enroll in foreign higher education (HE) programs and obtain qualifications offered by overseas providers without leaving home. The growing demand for tertiary education and the mounting demand for a skilled labor force, which could not be satisfied in some underdeveloped or developing countries, provide other reasons that account for this phenomenon (Altbach and Knight 2007). Thus, TNHE appears as an effective and efficient way to expand their HE sector (Huang 2007; Verbik and Merkley 2007). By 2024, it is expected that the number of mobile students globally will have surged to 3.85 million, an increase from 3.04 million in 2011 (British Council 2012), More importantly, the Asia-Pacific region will have become the top source of international students. According to an Organization for Economic Co-operation and Development (OECD) report entitled "Education Indicators in Focus," the largest number of international students come from China, India, and Korea, such that Asian student proportions accounting for 53 percent of all the mobile students worldwide in 2011 (OECD 2013). The British Council went further to predict that India and China will contribute 35 percent of global growth in the number of mobile students during the forecast period (namely, from 2011 to 2024) (British Council 2012).

China represents a good instance to demonstrate the fever for TNHE. With a strong commitment to transform its higher education system to become more international in the quest for increasing the global rankings of Chinese universities, together with the intention to diversify higher education learning experiences, the Chinese government has tried to incorporate new ideas and practices from overseas institutions, particularly encouraging the development of TNHE to change the HE landscape in mainland China. The number of transnational cooperation activities in China has increased tremendously, from two (Huang 2010) in 1995 to 1176 in 2016 (The Information Platform of Chinese-Foreign Cooperation in Running Schools,[1] 2016). During this period, the Chinese government has changed its attitude toward TNHE, from a tool to produce more HE opportunities to an effective method to improve national teaching and research qualities. The present study focuses on the strategies adopted by both the country and one Sino-foreign cooperation university as a case study, in assuring quality in Chinese transnational cooperation activities.

TNHE IN CHINA: QUALITY CONCERNS

The rapid development of TNHE in the past few decades has given rise to numerous problems such as the introduction of low-quality educational resources and programs and the repeated cooperative engagements within the same academic disciplines (with the most focus on business, economics, or accounting), all of which have occasioned various alerts from the central government. For example, The Ministry of Education (MOE) released a series of documents to review and standardize TNHE from 2004 to 2007. These were subsequently updated, but the basic manner in which the central government has chosen to deal with this population and its practices was established by these prior policies. The *Notice on Reviewing Transnational Cooperation Programs and Institutions* (the 2004 Notice), issued in 2004, requires all transnational cooperation programs and institutions to be reexamined. In accordance with the former promulgated policies, the *Regulations of the People's Republic of China on Chinese-Foreign Cooperation in Running Schools* (State Council 2003) and the *Implementation Measures of Regulations of the People's Republic of China on Chinese-Foreign Cooperation in Running Schools* (MOE 2004a), the cooperative activities that failed to meet the requirements prescribed by the Regulations would, within two years starting from the date of implementation of the Regulations, accomplish such requirements; for those that failed to do so within the prescribed time limit, the examination and approval authorities would dissolve them (State Council 2003, Article 63). The 2004 Notice devolved the power of review to local governments where the process of revision focuses on ten different aspects, including whether the programs or institutions involve military, religious, or political areas which are forbidden by the central government; whether the enrollment of students and the award of certificates conform to the relative laws; and whether the charge of these programs or institutions has been approved by the affected governments. In this Notice, local governments were required to report the results before March 31, 2005, to the Department of International Cooperation and Exchange, according to which the MOE would issue the certificate and approval to the qualified programs or institutions and dissolve the unqualified ones.

The 2004 Notice appeared as a turning point in the regulation of TNHE by the central government. After the expansion of the Chinese HE system, including the active participation of private and overseas educational providers, China has successfully transformed its HE system from the elite to the mass dimensions, to use Trow's well-known categories (Trow 1973), marked by its increasing enrollment rate of 17 percent by 2003 (UNESCO 2016). The central government thus could change its focus from increasing the enrollment rate to improving the teaching and research qualities, in order to tackle the problems accompanying this rapid expansion in the context of insufficient investment, which had led to a variety of poor outcomes such as the appearance of "degree mills". The 2004 Notice indicated the changing emphasis from quantity to quality, demonstrating that the Chinese government was prepared to recognize the gap between its higher education institutions (HEIs) and world-class universities overseas. The number of newly approved transnational cooperation activities dropped drastically after 2004, indicating that TNHE in China had entered the quality phase.

After releasing the 2004 Notice, the MOE issued two more documents to further regulate TNHE. The *Advice on Current Situation of TNHE* (the 2006 Advice), issued in 2006, re-emphasized the importance of high-quality educational resources to the country and pointed out that TNHE should be more sensitive to the demands of regional and national economic growth. In this regard, HEIs are encouraged to cooperate with overseas universities in the disciplines which are weak or lack capacity. The Advice also suggests that the central and western areas, those behind in providing higher education capacity, should pay more attention to promoting the development of TNHE (MOE 2006, Article 3). Concerning the quality assurance of TNHE, the MOE emphasizes the management of enrollment and the awarding of certification. The transnational cooperation programs or institutions should ensure that the prevailing academic standards are equal to or exceed those of the "sending" HEIs (degree-conferring programs for bachelor degrees or above) and that certificates should be fully recognized by the sending countries (MOE 2006, Article 4). The 2006 Advice also focuses on an institution's management in making academic appointments and in assessing the quality of foreign faculty. All of these developments demonstrated the Chinese government's determination to import world-class educational resources, thereby providing a practical and efficient way to improve academic quality and internationalize the Chinese HE system. However, the Advice fails to specify the agency that should take responsibility to regulate TNHE, an omission that renders all the items concerning quality assurance of little practical use. In addition, even while the MOE was aware of the issue of overcharging fees in TNHE, it offered no clear regulations in either the cost calculation or the setting of tuition.

Soon after the release of the 2006 Notice, the MOE issued another document to emphasize the standardization of TNHE, the *Notice on Further Standardizing TNHE* (the 2007 Document). The 2007 Document summarizes the reports covering the reviewing process conducted in 2004–2005, pointing out six main problems that emerged during the development of TNHE in China: repeated cooperation in low-cost disciplines (business, management, computer science, etc.); profit-driven activities; insufficient input of foreign educational resources; lowered enrollment criteria; various disorders in financial management; and illegal charges toward students (MOE 2007). To solve the above-mentioned problems, the 2007 Document stipulated that transnational cooperation programs or institutions should publicize their charge level, forbidding the HEIs to use TNHE as a method to generate excess profits (MOE 2007, Article 2). Noticing that some universities offer preparatory courses and claim that students graduating from this kind of courses could take credits which are recognized by the foreign partners and facilitate their continuing study overseas, the MOE clarified that preparatory courses are not part of TNHE as approved by the central government and forbids HEIs to use the label of TNHE to enroll students for these (MOE 2007, Article 5).

Realizing the asymmetric information pattern prevalent in the transnational educational market, the MOE started to build the official website (The Information Platform of Chinese-foreign Cooperation in Running Schools) to monitor TNHE and provide approved information for certificates/diplomas to be awarded by the transnational cooperation programs/institutions. The changing nature of the criteria to be utilized in approving TNHE is the most important and influential issue addressed in the 2007 Document. The MOE stipulates that the world ranking of the overseas HEIs and the quality of foreign faculty will be the pivotal factors in approving new transnational cooperation programs or institutions, and continued cooperation in the disciplines which have already been introduced or the charging of excessive tuition fees could not be approved (MOE 2007, Article 3).

The impact of these three documents on the development of TNHE was obvious. After the release of the 2004 Notice, the number of newly approved transnational cooperation activities decreased drastically. There were only four programs/institutions to gain approval in 2005, and in 2006, the number was 25. The 2006 Advice and 2007 Document also slowed the development of TNHE. The numbers were four in 2007, three in 2008, and only one in 2009 (Fig. 4.1).

The newest published policy, termed the *National Medium and Long-Term Educational Reform and Development Planning Outline* of 2010, has strengthened the importance of introducing world-class educational resources. Meanwhile, after a three-year experimental quality evaluation conducted in four provinces—Tianjin, Liaoning, Jiangsu, and Henan—from 2009 to 2016, the MOE promulgated the *Evaluating Plan of TNHE* to further assure the quality of TNHE (MOE, 2009–2016). The aforementioned plans require that all the transnational cooperation activities in China (except those which register as independent legal entities) that are approaching their validation dates must submit and publicize their self-reports. With reference to the results released by the MOE, this included 346 programs/second-tier colleges under evaluation in 2013. The qualified rate was 83 percent. All of these measures indicate the Chinese government's ambition to transform "the country from an economic power to a power with rich human resources" (Mok and Yu 2011, p. 241) and its increasing attention to the quality issue. The remainder of this chapter provides detailed information about how quality assurance procedures

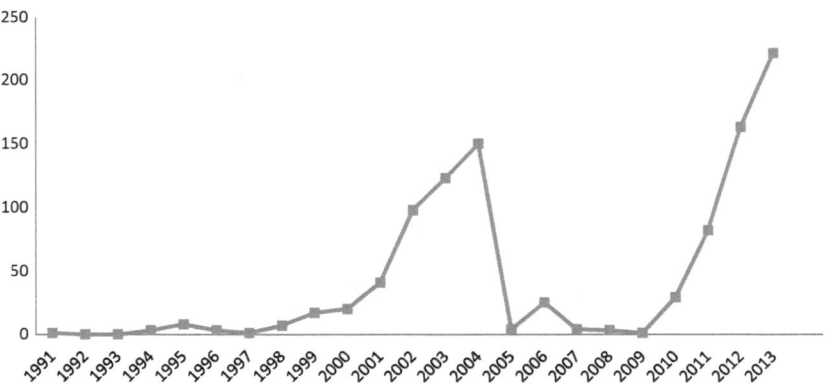

Fig. 4.1 The number of newly approved transnational cooperation activities by the MOE (1991–2013) (*Source*: The information platform of Chinese-Foreign Cooperation in Running Schools, calculated by the authors)

operate at the institutional level, taking one Sino-foreign cooperation university as the case study.

CASE STUDY: QUALITY ASSURANCE IN A SINO-FOREIGN COOPERATION UNIVERSITY

As one herald of TNHE in China, University C has already successfully operated for more than ten years. Its overseas collaborator is a high-quality tertiary education institution consisting of several colleges in different disciplines. By 2015, it had produced five cohorts of graduates, most of whom continue their studies overseas (over 90 percent in 2013). Our fieldwork conducted in 2014 revealed that the strict quality assurance method adopted by University C was highly praised by its graduates, regarding it as the main reason why they were able to be admitted by foreign universities after graduation. Unlike the other seven Sino-foreign cooperation universities in China, University C recruited all the administrative staff and faculty on its own instead of sharing some of the necessary human resources with either the Chinese or the foreign partners. However, the institution is also required to be supervised by a combination of both the Chinese government and the overseas collaborator, since it has the entitlement to issue Chinese and foreign diploma/certificates. On the basis of these two kinds of evaluation, University C has developed comprehensive and student-centered quality assurance system that is unusual and effective.

The evaluation conducted by the overseas collaborator consists primarily of three aspects: accreditation, an annual monitoring visit, and validation. To be more specific, the accreditation process focuses on the whole quality assurance procedure, deciding whether University C is qualified to issue the foreign diploma in the next round (five years). The items evaluated include strategic planning; review of the organization structure; regulatory information; adequacy and quality of staffing; the nature of student experiences; learning, teaching, and assessment, including learning resources; marketing and admission; macro statistical data; the partnership agreement; and relevant government documentation. Overall, the evaluation places less emphasis on quantitative data, utilizing a range of qualitative indicators to provide a richer portrait of the institution. For instance, with respect to the student experience, in-depth interviews are conducted with several students in order to gain a more comprehensive understanding of the range and nature of their feedback. After the evaluation, the overseas partner will publish a report and develop a plan in response to its findings, highlighting the problems that emerged during this process and outlining future possible improvements. Following the development of the report and the plan, the annual monitoring visit focuses on any deficiencies developed during the review. Finally, the validation exercise examines the quality of teaching procedures, covering the discipline/course design, syllabus revision, and examination methods.

Beyond this set of procedures, however, the Chinese government has not yet formulated comprehensive and specialized evaluation methods to ensure the quality in Sino-foreign cooperation universities even though TNHE has been in a process of development in China for three decades. University C, unlike other public HEIs, is only requested to undergo the evaluation of the MOE on several dimensions such as the accreditation and review of campus facilities, rather than be subject to the direct monitoring and management of the MOE. From an overall perspective, the evaluation of the Chinese government mainly focuses on four perspectives. The first is with reference to the application of the *Regulations of the People's Republic of China on Academic Degrees* (MOE 1980) and the *Temporary Implementation of the Regulations of the People's Republic of China on Academic Degrees* (MOE 1981). Within these frameworks, the MOE is in charge of assessing whether the students' academic performance and graduation theses meet the criteria required for the issuance of Chinese degrees. The second set of standards, the *Criteria for Chinese Higher Education Institutions' Facility (Temporary)* (MOE 2004b), requires University C to satisfy the requirements of running a Chinese HEI, such as retaining an appropriate student–faculty ratio and meeting the qualifications established for faculty and the computers/dormitory/teaching apparatus. A third requirement is that University C should undertake the *evaluation of undergraduate programs on teaching quality* across seven aspects: the guiding ideology, faculty component, teaching facilities and utilities, curriculum design, teaching management, student instructions, and teaching performances. The last but not least requirement is that University C should apply for the approval of the MOE before opening any new degree programs and for deciding the annual enrollment quota.

To conclude, the evaluation methods undertaken by the overseas collaborator and Chinese government are illustrated in Table 4.1:

Based on the evaluation required by the overseas partner and the Chinese government, University C has developed its own quality assurance mechanism as displayed in Fig. 4.2.

Table 4.1 Quality assurance methods of overseas collaborator and the Chinese government

Evaluation methods	Ideology	Teaching plan	Teaching procedure	Teaching evaluation
Overseas collaborator				
Accreditation	Strategic planning	Strategic planning, staffing, learning resources, marketing and admission, partnership agreement and government documentation	Organization structure, regulatory information, student experience, learning, teaching and assessment	Teaching and assessment, statistic data
Annual monitoring visit	Targeting the existing problems and check the follow-up improvements			
Validation		Discipline design, syllabus, academic development		Examinations
The Chinese government				
The evaluation of undergraduate programs on teaching quality	University orientation, administrative function, talent cultivating	Faculty, teaching facilities and utilities, curriculum design	Teaching management, student instructions	Ideology and morality education, physical and aesthetics education, employment
Accreditation		Curriculum design		Academic performance, graduation thesis
Basic facilities		Faculty, library, living conditions, equipment		
Approval		Degree programs		

Source: Developed by the authors

Figure 4.2 elaborates the process for the quality assurance mechanism which University C regards as basic for a qualified education institution. First, the university places great emphasis on enrolling talented candidates, deciding the critical admission criterion should be candidates from the first level (*yiben xian*), and requiring applicants to undergo an extra examina-

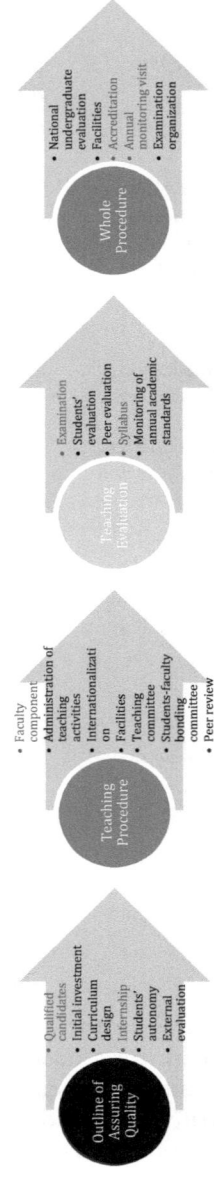

Fig. 4.2 The quality assurance mechanism in University C (*Source:* Developed by the authors)

tion before they can be finally admitted to University C. Second, strongly supported by the local government to which it responds, both financially and politically, the initial funding of University C has been, to some extent, sufficient to establish it as a world-class HEI. They have assured the creation of advanced laboratories and offered a globally competitive salary structure to attract prestigious faculty. Third, since University C can freely design the content of its curriculum, it can determine the selection of materials used in the courses, and teaching and examination methods, all of which permit University C to cater to its students' needs. In addition, the university has attempted to explore a greater number of internship opportunities and to encourage students to be more involved in the daily affairs of the education process, such as the evaluation of teaching quality, the purchase of professional books, and the evaluation of teaching facilities. And last but not least, besides the conduct of an internal peer review through the evaluations conducted by the overseas collaborator and the Chinese government, University C has invited an external examination committee to review teaching with the goal of ensuring its quality as required by QAA (the Quality Assurance Agency for Higher Education, which is responsible for the quality insurance and improvement of overseas provision of UK higher education[2]). The quality assurance mechanism (Fig. 4.2) offers comprehensive details for the quality assurance procedure. Furthermore, realizing the vital role played by teaching activities in a qualified HEI, University C has developed through various schedules the means to guarantee effective and efficient instructional capacity for classes.

Specifically, University C has set up its own selection criteria to recruit world-renowned faculty, as a prerequisite for ensuring qualified teaching activities. From the administrative perspective, University C has clarified the boundary between executive power and academic autonomy, devolving more discretionary power to the faculty in the conduct of its teaching and research. In addition, as one Sino-foreign cooperative university, University C benefits from its collaboration with foreign HEIs for internationalizing the students' learning experience. For instance, University C has adopted the norm of small-size class settings, encouraging more interaction between teachers and students, and aiming to cultivate within students the capacity to become active learners. The university also has established a students–faculty liaison committee, facilitating students in their communication with the specific teachers when they encounter difficulties.

With respect to teaching evaluations, except for the annual monitoring visit and the design of syllabi as discussed previously, the methods for conducting final examinations represent another innovation of University C. The examination paper developed by the responsible teacher(s) is required to be submitted to audit of the appropriate university faculty and the overseas collaborator before it may be put into use. The marked examination papers will also be randomly inspected by the external examiners from other overseas universities (which have no direct relationship to the two collaborating ones) or in some cases even from other Chinese HEIs. Although this results in a time-consuming process, the relative cost is considered justified by the perception of fairness for the examination, which is promoted by the practice.

In a word, University C is required, under the evaluation of the MOE, to assess its undergraduate teaching quality and facilities, and to undergo a parallel assessment by its overseas partner and QAA to gain a certificate-conferring accreditation of which the annual monitoring visit of teaching quality is a part. Beyond this, the university itself developed a distinct examination process, employing external examiners to ensure both teaching and research qualities. The combination of the different evaluation methods, to some extent, warrants the high quality perception of University C. As one of the eight Sino-foreign cooperation universities, it has gained strong support from its local government, like the other seven HEIs. However, the investment from the government has been mainly focused on the establishment of the physical campus or the creation of facilities, which subsequently, along with daily operational expenses, are to be sustained primarily by student tuition fees. Without a stable appropriation from the central government, University C has been influenced more by the force of the market and the spirit of free competition, when compared with similar Chinese public HEIs. Indeed, the author's primary interviewee on the campus confirmed that financial pressure is indeed one of the reasons why they cherish the fame of their perceived quality education and the positive regard it gains them.

CONCLUSION

After three decades of development, TNHE has been recognized as an increasingly important and indispensable part of the build out and maturation of the Chinese HE system. During this process, the MOE has re-centralized its control toward TNHE twice. First, the standardization of TNHE by the MOE from 2004 to 2007 demonstrated the resolution of the central government in introducing high-quality education resources, representing the changing emphasis of the national government in the shift from providing higher education capacity as it moved into its rapid early massification stage, to that of creating and assuring quality. Following that, the MOE has taken the further step to ensure the quality of the established cooperation programs/second-tier colleges by suspending or canceling the disqualified ones. It is still too early to reach a final verdict that the exemption of the evaluation for the Sino-foreign cooperation universities fully illustrates the trust of the central government toward these eight joint-venture universities. Only the passage of more time will confirm that view.

In confronting the impact of globalization with the resultant dimensions of increasing massification as it has impacted the internationalization of the Chinese HE system, the central government seems to have been significantly influenced by neo-liberalism in the creation a relatively free regulatory environment for the eight Sino-foreign cooperation universities to compete with each other. However, within a retrospective view of the nature of the policy environment created by the MOE, whether the autonomy enjoyed by these joint-venture universities in quality assurance aspect could and will continue still remains a question mark for future researchers.

Notes

1. For more details, refer to http://www.crs.jsj.edu.cn/.
2. For more details, refer to http://www.qaa.ac.uk/reviews-and-reports/how-we-review-higher-education/review-of-overseas-provision.

References

Altbach, P. G., & Knight, J. (2007). The internationalization of higher education: Motivations and realities. *Journal of Studies in International Education, 11*(3–4), 290–305.

British Council. (2012). *The future of the world's mobile students to 2024.* Available online at: Retrieved June 4, 2016, from https://ei.britishcouncil.org/educationintelligence/future-world-mobile-students-2024.

Global Alliance for Transnational Education. (1999). *Trade in transnational education services.* Boston: Global Alliance for Transnational Education.

Huang, F. (2007). Internationalization of higher education in the developing and emerging countries: A focus on transnational higher education in Asia. *Journal of Studies in International Education, 11*(3–4), 421–432.

Huang, F. (2010). Transnational higher education in Japan and China: A comparative study. In D. W. Chapman, W. K. Cummings, & G. A. Postiglione (Eds.), *Crossing borders in East Asian higher education* (pp. 265–282). Hong Kong: The University of Hong Kong.

Knight, J. (2006). Programmes, providers and accreditors on the move: Implications for the recognition of qualifications. In A. Rauhvargers & S. Bergan (Eds.), *Recognition in the Bologna process: Policy development and the road to good practice* (pp. 139–160). Strasbourg: Council of Europe Publishing.

Ministry of Education (MOE). (1980). *The regulations of the People's Republic of China on academic degrees* (in Chinese). Available online at: Retrieved June 4, 2016, from http://www.moe.edu.cn/publicfiles/business/htmlfiles/moe/moe_619/200407/1315.html.

Ministry of Education (MOE). 1981. *The temporary implementation of the regulations of the People's Republic of China on academic degrees* (in Chinese). Available online at: Retrieved June 4, 2016, from http://www.moe.edu.cn/publicfiles/business/htmlfiles/moe/moe_620/200409/3133.html.

Ministry of Education (MOE). (2004a). *The implementation measures of the regulations of the People's Republic of China on Chinese-foreign cooperation in running schools* (in Chinese). Available online at: Retrieved June 4, 2016, from http://www.MoE.gov.cn/publicfiles/business/htmlfiles/MoE/MoE_162/200408/2544.html.

Ministry of Education (MOE). (2004b). *The Criteria for Chinese higher education institutions' facility (temporary)* (in Chinese). Available online at: Retrieved June 4, 2016, from http://www.moe.edu.cn/publicfiles/business/htmlfiles/moe/s7050/201412/xxgk_180515.html.

Ministry of Education (MOE). (2006). *The advice on current situation of TNHE* (in Chinese). Available online at: Retrieved June 4, 2016, from http://www.crs.jsj.edu.cn/index.php/default/news/index/1.

Ministry of Education (MOE). (2007). *The notice on further standardizing TNHE* (in Chinese). Available online at: Retrieved June 4, 2016, from http://www.crs.jsj.edu.cn/index.php/default/news/index/18.

Ministry of Education (MOE). (2009–2016). *The plan for TNHE evaluation* (in Chinese). Available online at: Retrieved June 4, 2016, from http://www.cfce.cn/a/pinggu/.

Mok, K. H., & Yu, K. M. (2011). The quest for regional education hub status and transnational higher education: Challenges for managing human capital in Asia. *Asia Pacific Journal of Education, 31*(3), 229–248.

Organization for Economic Co-operation and Development (OECD). (2013). *Education indicators in focus.* Available online at: Retrieved June 4, 2016, from http://www.oecd.org/education/skills-beyond-school/EDIF%202013-N%C2%B014%20(eng)-Final.pdf.

State Council. (2003). *Regulations of the People's Republic of China on Chinese-foreign cooperation in running schools* (in Chinese). Available online at: Retrieved June 4, 2016, from http://www.jsj.edu.cn.

Trow, M. (1973). *Problems in the transition from elite to mass higher education.* Berkeley: Carnegie Commission on Higher Education.

United Nations Educational, Scientific, and Cultural Organization (UNESCO). (2016). *Database.* Available online at: Retrieved on June 4, 2016, from http://data.uis.unesco.org/?queryid=142.

United Nations Educational, Scientific, and Cultural Organization (UNESCO) and Council of Europe. (2001). *The UNESCO-CEPES/Council of Europe code of good practice for the provision of transnational education.* Paris: UNESCO.

Verbik, L., & Merkley, C. (2007). The international branch campus: Models and trends. *International Higher Education, 46,* 14–15.

CHAPTER 5

Creative Moments in Company: A Quality Pursuing Case of an International Graduate Education Program in a Chinese University

Hong Zhu and Nneoma Grace L. Egbuonu

BACKGROUND OF STUDY

In the context of massification and internationalization of higher education, Chinese universities are attempting to move from a peripheral to a more central position in the global educational community (Hayhoe and Liu 2010) with China reaching out to attract international students. In 2010, the Chinese government announced "National Guidelines for Medium- and Long-term Educational Reform and Development (2010–2020)" (Ministry of Education of the People's Republic of China 2010, cited in Zhu 2011) and expressed its determination to become the Asian destination that attracts the largest number of international students within ten years (China Association for International Education, CAFSA 2010, ibid.). Between 2010 and 2014, China enrolled a total of 1.6 million international students. According to official statistics (MOE 2016), in 2015, the number of international students studying in China reached 397,635 (Fig. 5.1).

H. Zhu (✉) • N.G.L. Egbuonu
Faculty of Education, Northeast Normal University,
Changchun, Jilin, China

© The Author(s) 2017
D.E. Neubauer, C. Gomes (eds.),
Quality Assurance in Asia-Pacific Universities,
DOI 10.1007/978-3-319-46109-0_5

71

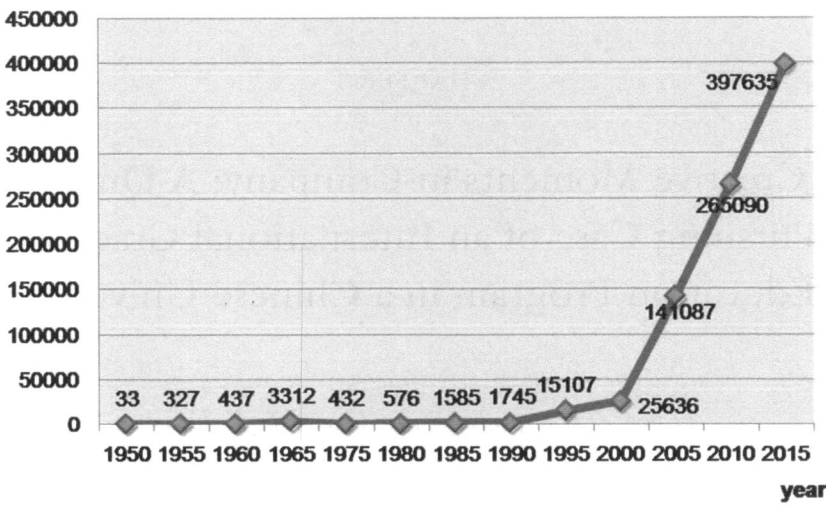

Fig. 5.1   Increase of international students in China from 1950 to 2015

The changes in Chinese higher education with respect to international students in China have extended well beyond increases in student numbers through expansion in the diversity of source countries, the forms of funding developed for supporting such engagements, expansion in the number of academic areas seeking international students, and the diversity of instructional languages. Overall, these changes can be viewed as relevant examples of one aspect of the massification of Chinese higher education that are not limited to a mere increase in numbers.

Chinese universities are making efforts in moving toward the center of the international higher education society (Hayhoe and Liu 2010). However, compared with many developed countries, China still lags behind in both the quantity and the quality of its inbound international students (UNESCO 2010, cited in Zhu and Ma 2011). In order to catch up with the world-class universities in both the quantity and quality of inbound international students, the Ministry of Education of China has depicted a long-term vision in its "National Guidelines for Medium- and

Long-term Educational Reform and Development 2010–2020" that emphasizes the following:

- a further increase in the enrollment of inbound international students;
- an increase in the quantity of Chinese government-funded scholarships, focusing on funding students from developing countries;
- the expansion of full foreign language instruction academic programs at tertiary levels; and
- persistent improvement in the quality of foreign students' education.

It is instructive to inquire how the medium- and long-term visions have been put in practice, specifically how the quality of international student education has been persistently improved. These elements are significant to both policy research and practice in higher education. The chapter illustrates the efforts in pursuit of higher education quality made by practitioners in a major Chinese university and discusses the implications of such an experience.

THE CASE OF NORTH UNIVERSITY

The study reported on in this chapter was carried out at North University (NU) (a pseudonym). Established in 1946, NU is a comprehensive university funded and administered by the Ministry of Education. NU is comprised of 19 schools, 56 undergraduate programs, and a graduate school. The graduate school offers 147 master's degree programs and 78 doctoral degree programs.

NU started receiving international students in the late 1960s at the very beginning of the period of higher education massification in China. Since 2003, the number of international students in NU has grown significantly. By 2015, NU had hosted about 10,042 international students from about 90 countries and regions. Among them the number of international students studying for academic degrees has continued to grow steadily (Fig. 5.2).

In the fall of 2008, NU started providing full English instruction graduate degree programs, which are authorized and funded mainly by the Ministry of Education. Under this NU project, the Faculty of Education began its full English instruction program for international graduate students (MA, PhD, and visiting scholars)[1] in the same year. By 2015, the

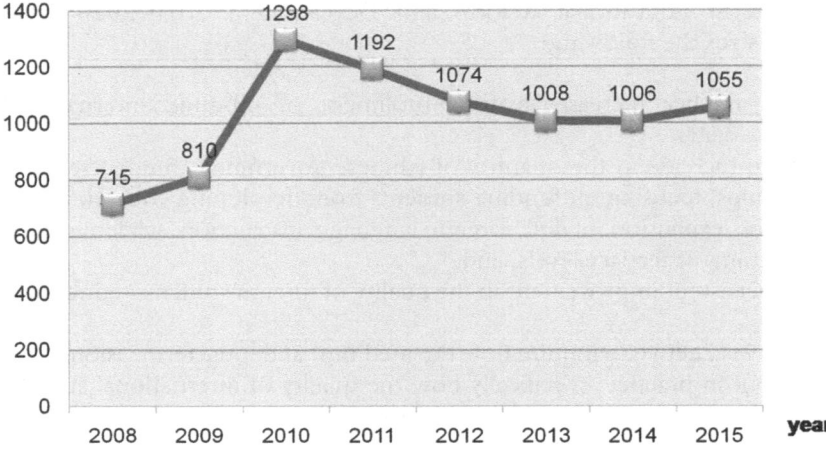

Fig. 5.2 Numbers of International Students in NU

faculty of education had hosted 178 full-time students from 41 countries. Of the 178 students, 119 of them studied in the full English instruction graduate study program (Fig. 5.3).

CHALLENGES AND STRATEGIES FOR QUALITY

Two important interrelated challenges exist for this program focused on international students matriculating within an English language program. Each in its own way requires approaches that tend to stand outside the "conventional" pathways into content courses within graduate education. The first is the need to develop a classroom culture with sufficient strength and yet flexibility to accommodate students from such diverse backgrounds. Although each enters the program having passed entry-levels requirements in English language,[2] the practical diversity that exists within their prior language training is great inasmuch (as expected) different countries with their own distinct higher education systems pursue language training with diverse methodologies and levels of rigor. The challenge for the NU program is to develop a variety of means with sufficient complexity to accommodate these differences and relatively quickly

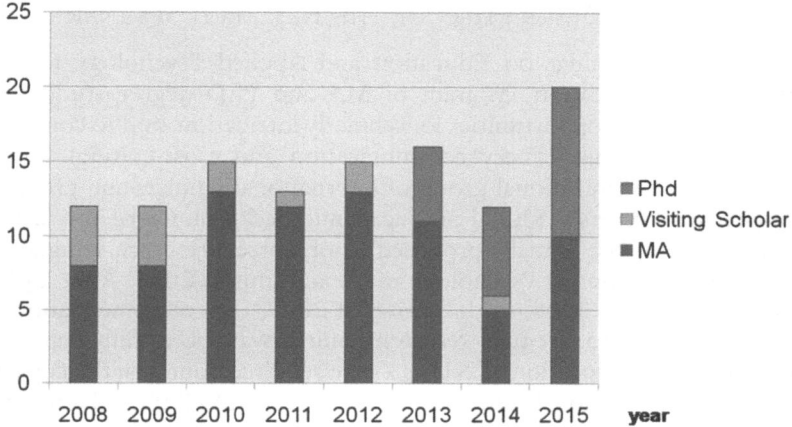

Fig. 5.3 NU Education Faculty, 2008–2015

establish a classroom culture that can promote the goals of the program itself. Beyond this is the realization that given the differences between cohorts year by year, the "lessons learned" at the classroom level for each cohort must be challenged and proved viable for each subsequent cohort.

The second challenge is to accept the fact that the "chemistry" of each cohort will differ, and year by year, it is necessary to fashion a pedagogy that allows for a process of increasing linguistic acquisition as well as a culture of effective group interaction. This latter challenge is both considerable in its very nature (again given the difference in training and background of each cohort)[3] and one that is inherently dynamic given the very different nature of each individual cohort. In practice, the variety of professional experience of the teaching staff of the faculty of education at NU allows the program to create a dynamic balance of situational-specific practices for each cohort that necessarily is tailored in some degree for that cohort itself. Various strategies have been adopted to cope with these challenges. For the purpose of discussing academic quality pursuit, this chapter has chosen to illustrate a most significant example based on a research seminar approach used in this program.

A Brief Description of the Research Seminar

The Research Seminar on Education and Applied Psychology for the International Education Program of MA and PhD degree students is designed to create opportunities for scholarly interaction, and to construct a bridge of interdisciplinary communication and cross-cultural understanding. An organizational group of international scholars and graduate students with diverse cultural and academic backgrounds of the faculty of education of NU initially proposed to organize a research seminar on Education and Applied Psychology in the autumn of 2008. After a pilot of one semester in 2008, in the spring of 2009, the recommendation to convert the pilot to a regular research seminar was successfully approved by the faculty of education of NU as a core required course of the curriculum of the International Education Program for MA/PhD and advanced studies of NU.

Supervised by core faculty members of the faculty of education, the research seminar is administered by the seminar committee, which consists of volunteers from the program. Since 2008, the research seminar has successfully hosted over 180 sessions. The seminars cover a wide range of topics: education, psychology, culture, art and music, as well as exploring other important issues related to education. The speakers providing input to the seminars are from more than 40 countries from Africa, America (North and South), Asia, and Europe.

Over the past eight years, the seminar has been constructed with a particular focus on the culture of professionalism and cross-cultural exchange. It is continuing to serve as a communication platform for ongoing events and undertakings in education studies at NU and beyond. The immediate aim of the seminar is to serve our students' individual research agendas and create a forum for intensive interaction on larger interdisciplinary questions related to the study carried out by our MA and PhD students and visiting scholars. Beyond these goals, the seminar is open to other researchers and scholars willing to share their academic and cultural experiences, in ways that focus on their significance for education in its broader senses.

The seminar is organized around five primary modules that encompass Applied Psychology (Education and Culture); Curriculum and Pedagogy: Educational Theory and Policy (Management); Higher Education and Comparative Education; and Teacher Education and Teacher Professional Development. The seminar itself is structured around a set of common procedures created and overseen by the seminar committee that vary in practice from instance to instance, but in general follow a common form. Within this process, each individual participant is assigned to one or more modules based on the nature of his/her presentation topics. The seminar committee, comprised of representatives from multiple disciplines, contributes to both the organization and the operation of the seminar by inviting and reviewing proposals, creating an overall schedule for the complete semester, and allocating duties among program members. These include preparing and posting the seminar posters, chairing individual seminars, ushering the audience and timing the presentation, in addition to collecting and summarizing feedback for individual speakers. In the spring semester of 2016, the seminar committee introduced and included a new role—that of a discussant at the stage of thesis proposal and defense rehearsals. It requires both MA and PhD candidates to invite a senior colleague to review their proposal/thesis and give comments on their work to initiate the discussion in the seminar. Unfortunately, due to the deadline of this book, feedback on the role of discussants is not yet available for this new role.

The requirements for the seminar are established well in advance and made known to all participants during the program orientation. As such, in its current form, it is a required course that provides two credits for successful conclusion and is graded pass/fail. Members are required to attend all the sessions consistently in the first academic year and participate in most of the sessions in subsequent academic years. Each member is required to present once a semester in their first year, and those who pursue a degree are required to present a review of their academic work (such as literature reviews, proposals, and thesis/dissertation defense rehearsals). All members are also required to undertake particular tasks as mandated by the seminar committee (e.g. chairing, discussing, posting, ushering, timing, collecting, and summarizing feedback).

Pursuing Quality Within the Research Seminar

It is the nature of higher education structure within Chinese institutions that all courses are expected to be framed and conducted with respect to broad definitions of quality that have been determined at the ministry level. Granting this framework for quality, individual faculty, especially those operating within an interdisciplinary environment, are impelled to raise the issue of how these broad, generalized notions of quality can be made sensible at the micro level of the classroom. This is especially a relevant issue when the "subject" and the "classroom environment" in question are complicated by issues such as the diversity of student backgrounds and the inherently different teaching styles of an interdisciplinary classroom. This structural distinction can be seen to have two "faces" as it were. On the one hand, it can be seen that quality as defined at the macro level is not subject to direct inquiry and change, while on the other hand, the implementation of such strictures at the micro level is always and necessarily a matter of interpretation of higher-level standards.

QUALITY OF HIGHER EDUCATION AND THE ANALYTIC FRAMEWORK

Much as Neubauer, Hawkins and Gomes argue in Chapter One of this volume, in virtually every educational environment, practitioners will have an intuitive sense of quality within a given setting and no doubt seek to pursue that. The critical and enduring issue at the classroom level for the practitioner is ensuring that this intuitive sense aligns with some broader dimension of quality that can be practiced and justified within a given setting.

This is no less true for the whole of an institution, which shares both a formal notion of quality and its many diverse exemplifications within individual classrooms. Within my own environment I understand quality within education as both a curricular and a pedagogical process that results from the cultivation of students within a culture of limited autonomy, which implies in turn integrity of personality, knowledge, and capacity by the instructor and through structured engagements an acceptance by students as well. In other words, the quality of education resides in relative student autonomy, the pursuit of an integrated person with the knowledge and ability to live a self-determined life. While as a practitioner I am still at the starting point of exploring these qualities on a personal level, this predisposition on my part is derived in turn from my educational experience in both the United States and Canada[4] as well as my teaching experience in China. Overall, I have been considering the quality of higher education from two perspectives: the requirement and expectation that the instructor is qualified by both training and predisposition for the educational experience involved and that he/she is capable of regarding the study as a full-fledged member of the teaching relationship.

In this regard I have been much influenced by the elements summarized by Marshall for such a relationship (drawn from a variety of paradigmatic elements situated within various philosophies of self), namely, the maintenance of the integrity of the self (psychology), the doctrine that the human will carry within his/her own guiding principle (philosophy); the right or power of self-government (political science); and the idea of the self-determining social actor (sociology). (Marshall 1998).

At a formal level, the seminar is governed by an explicit set of expectations for all participants, whether they are following the MA or the PhD track. These are to conduct a research project (MA thesis and PhD dissertation) that seeks to constitute original work independently accomplished and success in the conduct of an oral examination in defense of the project. The conduct of the program is also strongly focused on the goal of ensuring that the graduate is qualified for competitive employment opportunities and encompasses teaching, research, and service, and that the candidate is realistically qualified for such employment tasks. Within the seminar structure, attention is paid to ensuring that candidates are qualified in what are viewed as the primary domains of knowledge, ability, and skills in both conceptual and empirical domains that may be readily transferable to employment within quality higher education environments. In practice, this leads to assessments in the range and quality of knowledge for both a specific subject and across interdisciplinary boundaries. Here the assessments seek to determine whether individuals possess in-depth knowledge and understanding of both the subject and its methodology(ies), a critical awareness of current issues and development of the particular domain of scholarship, and some vision of how international developments are taking place within education as a whole.

An individual's abilities are reviewed across a broad spectrum, including the ability to study independently; to conceptualize, design, and implement a significant research project; to use a range of techniques and research methods applicable to scholarship demands of a particular subject; to initiate and take responsibility within a variety of circumstances; to solve problems in creative and innovative ways; to make decisions in challenging situations; to engage in a process of lifelong learning deemed suitable for professional development and personal growth; to cooperate and work collaboratively in a team; and (of particular importance for this particular program) to communicate effectively in various multicultural and international contexts.

At the skill level, students in the program are encouraged to develop a range of research methods (including literature review, data collecting and analyzing, and proposal and thesis writings), to acquire linguistic and intercultural communicative skills, to be able to develop and give presentations (expressing and listening), to become knowledgeable about various techniques (including various software skills) applicable to research and teaching, and to acquire teamwork skills (negotiation, collaboration, and cooperation).

The dominant premise to these methods is that their overall integration will begin the process of developing a "quality" scholar, defined in these instances as a critical and creative researcher, logical presenter and good listener, a tolerant and empathetic cultural learner, a cooperative team worker, and a visionary leader.

As reviewed above, the framework of quality for this study is categorized in Table 5.1:

Major Observations of Value

The research seminar is designed to enhance the quality of the program by creating opportunities for students to hone their academic skills, acquire cross-cultural and disciplinary knowledge, and cultivate the spirit of autonomy. The best way to know about the effects of the design is to inquire from the stakeholders: precisely put, these are the students. Therefore, to evaluate the seminar, I conducted an interview in April 2015, sampling 18 participants from the program's students. They are registered MA (12) and PhD (6) students of the program from 11 countries (Cambodia, Ghana, Greece, Lesotho, Nigeria, Pakistan, Russia, Thailand, Tanzania, Thailand, and Zambia). The interview focused around three main research questions:

1. What are the expectations of international students in the full English education program?

Table 5.1 The framework of "quality"

	Knowledge	Ability	Skills
Research			
Teach			
Service			

2. What are students' practices in the research seminar?
3. What do these practices mean to respondents regarding academic quality?

All the interviews were recorded and transcribed. The transcript texts were coded on the basis of the quality and analytical framework reviewed above.

All the interviewees expressed the commitment that they expected to complete their postgraduate study. After graduation, they wished to work in a university or an education institute/organization, or continue their course of academic study. Therefore, they expect to obtain the knowledge and acquire the abilities described above in section three.

The research seminar from which the findings were drawn meets with weekly regularity, and given its nature as an accredited student autonomous research seminar supervised by a faculty member at any given point in time, it constitutes an innovative experience for all the participants. In such seminars, participants are asked to play roles as audience, presenter, and organizer. Feedback on their experience and benefits regarding academic quality from the seminar includes an array of qualities known as "ADAM," which stands for Autonomy, Democracy across cultural and interdisciplinary vision, and Mentorship support.

The following details these qualities:

- **Autonomy and Democracy**

The seminar committees on which students serve are constructed voluntarily. However, in the encouraging and friendly multicultural learning environment nurtured, every participant (including both PhD and MA students, as well as visiting scholars) of the program will have an opportunity of sitting on a committee. Therefore, the research seminar is in effect and in an important sense completely derived from the students, by the students, and for the students. All decisions will have been discussed with the members and finalized through a democratic approach. This is a challenging task often for people from different countries with varying political, cultural, and religious backgrounds. English is used as an international instructional language albeit with different accents and even pragmatically different meanings and connotations. In practice, reaching decisions by the committee often involves many rounds of discussion, negotiation, and compromises before a consensual decision is reached. It benefits students by providing an arena to perform both as a leader and as a democratic participant. After sitting in the committee for one semester, one MA student reflected on her growth as a leader:

> As a leader, I got the positive idea that we are the collection of people from every corner of the world so we should cooperate and help each other. We are comprised of PhD and Master students but we should help each other [rather] than differentiating... we should know about our duties and responsibilities during the seminar sessions. (Katty,[5] MA, from Cambodia)

This view was echoed by many others.

> I've never had this [*sic*] kind of discussions before. In Russia we, students, didn't have any seminar of that kind of format, and we lacked an opportunity to speak, discuss and share. Also at our seminar [in NU] we have people from many countries all over the world. Additionally, the seminar has a kind of autonomy. It is ruled by students, and that kind of experience I didn't have at the Russian university (formal curricula). (Fleur, PhD student, from Russia)

The seminar's responsibilities and duties are equally allocated among students regardless of their relative status as PhD, MA, or visiting scholars. At the beginning, some students were not used to the practice of having a shared responsibility between PhD and MA students. But with the passage of time they witnessed the benefits of a democratic participation in the seminar and began to enjoy it. For example, Rajif, a PhD student, after almost six months' experience recognized:

> We are comprised of PhD and Master students but we should help each other rather than differentiating each other on the basis of program. We should know about our duties and responsibilities during the research seminar sessions. (Rajif, PhD student, from Pakistan)

• Cross-cultural and interdisciplinary vision

The seminar is designed to give students opportunities to explore a variety of engagements by creating a common cultural experience of sharing during the first year to their final thesis research exploration. Each seminar session follows the format of an international conference presentation: a

20-min. presentation, followed by a 10- to 15-min. question-and-answer engagement. The format challenges students to express themselves within the 20-min. framework and to practice how to question other present-ers critically and diplomatically. Meanwhile, listening, note taking, and explaining skills are also exercised.

An extract can give a developmental example of how this works for individual members:

> I had three presentations[6] during my participation in the research seminar. First was about native people from the region of Russia I live in. I wanted to show to the audience that Russia has a diverse population, different ethnic groups, and multicultural society. The second presentation was about a student club "Model United Nations organization." I wanted to talk about my personal experience in this organization, what impact it had on my life, my education. The last time I presented about my research interest—citizenship education. I wanted to share the information that I found interesting and challenge the way I was thinking about some democracy concepts. (Irven, Russia, after two-year MA study, in PhD 1st year)

As many of the interview subjects commented, through the presentation and question-answer series, they had obtained a wide variety of skills and abilities, including the opportunity to be critical about academic issues and subjects and the ability to organize their thoughts in a useful and informative manner. These occurrences contributed overall to a growth in confidence and an expanded scope in the subjects and perspectives that individuals were willing to present. The combination of these experiences contributed to a personal sense of confidence and an expanded scope of interest and knowledge. These arose in part from the opportunity to learn new things from different fields and the acquisition of new presentation skills such as working with power point presentations and getting familiar with "aca-demic" structures of speech and presentation. A major gain emphasized by several respondents was the acquisition of questioning skills and learning appropriate manners for doing so, for example, posing questions, listening, and making helpful comments. (Summarized from MA and PhD student respondents from Tanzania, Ghana, Cambodia, Pakistan, and Nigeria.)

- **Mentorship support**

One important aspect of the engagement elements of the seminar is that of mentorship. Although this was not a specific focus of the interview questions, the salience of it came through the interview data. Mentorship is, of course, one significant quality component of faculty and academic career development. Respondents here commented that they were able to obtain a strong sense of mentoring from the seminar that tended to emerge when they supported each other in what for many was an unfamiliar role.

As one student expressed her feeling in this regard: "it is [a] supportive, stimulating environment with excellent supervision, a strong community, like-minded students and teachers who provide mutual support." (Fleur, Russia, 1st year after two years of study for MA in the program)

However, another respondent offered the feedback that the seminar was not critical enough, though he enjoyed the tolerant culture: "Here there is more tolerance, tendency to sugar every presentation but academics [are] supposed to be critical" (Ketti, PhD student from Tanzania).

In fact, the seminar culture that has emerged is one in which senior participants have acquired a sense of mentoring, not only to participate actively themselves but also to leave room for the new comers to grow. As Cathy explained:

> After a lot of hard work preparing a presentation, most presenters (myself included) will want to get some form of constructive criticism. Not getting any or getting only negative feedback can be discouraging so I try my best to encourage an atmosphere of constructive criticism after presentations... There are times that I hold back from making my contributions in order to give room for other participants who do not contribute often to do so. In situations where no one brings up the aspects that I noted then I go on to contribute...I feel that there are students who may want to contribute but need some time to work up the confidence to do so. Also some contributions are not going to be unique to me alone so I like to give room for some other participant who seldom speaks to grab the opportunity. (Nigeria, PhD 1st year after a two-year MA in the program)

Mentoring,[7] or the giving of mutual support, has become a tradition and culture of this program such that senior students share their experience and provide guidance for newcomers in both academic learning and administrating activities.

• Intercultural learning and academic friendship

As a result of its openness to diversity of culture and disciplines, many participants have come from different schools and programs (e.g. Chinese programs in the faculty of education, school of business, biology, history, and from other universities because we post out on campus and open to the public), where they did not have seminars of this form (i.e. English speaking, student autonomous, and interdisciplinary). Participants from other schools brought different visions to our program, and the research expertise shown in our seminars also expanded their own scope of interest and experience. As diverse parts have been integrated into an overall whole, all participants benefit from a broadened vision of education in an international context. As one Greek student (in the Chinese BA program) expressed:

> The seminar is based [on] education subjects. And I have ... in the first place I didn't have interest in education. ... I'm getting more interested in education. [I thought] after graduating to study education. Because I want to mix history and education. I want to teach in university.

Interaction from diverse cultural, language, and academic backgrounds gives challenges to all participants but also cultivates participants' tolerance of difference and develops empathy for each other. As Fleur (cited above) commented:

> Communicating with students and professors from different cultural backgrounds can be both challenging and very rewarding. So that's why tolerance is one the most important factors in the multicultural class.

Learning across culture through interaction and cooperation, particularly by serving on the committee, has expanded students' vision and honed their skills to embrace differences and become comfortable working with people of different backgrounds. As one PhD student recalled:

> Sometimes it's difficult to deal with people, because of misunderstandings or different points of views. I experienced that everyone fights for and defend[s] his/her own ideas and sometimes it makes them blind to see and hear others. What I learned is that we need to be open-minded, not be spoiled by our pride or ego, and respect each other; we need to learn how to be objective and resolve conflicts diplomatically. What I also understood is that though we are from different cultures, the problems we face during cooperation with others are the same as everywhere. We have stereotypes, prejudices, we don't like to be judged and criticized and sometimes we don't react adequately. We need to learn how to work with others. And

by that I mean not only to understand others, but to realize, that we don't need to do everything independently. We need to learn how to trust each other, and not [be] afraid to divide responsibilities, how to convince people to be responsible and accountable. (Lametuz, PhD 1st year, from Thailand)

Our students love the research seminar. It is also well known throughout NU and among some universities in the general vicinity. I would love to end this finding section with two episodes that happened this week when I was writing this paragraph. A once-regular seminar participant from the school of music of NU told me:

Laoshi (teacher), your seminar has spread to our school! I helped my supervisor to organize one exactly like yours. We have had over one hundred sessions now. I wish I had kept attending yours so that I would be able to communicate in English, but ... (a Chinese PhD candidate of the school of music of NU; their seminar is in Chinese language)

The other episode comes from the latest PhD proposal defense rehearsal. After all four PhD students finished their presentations and discussions of their work, a Chinese instruction program PhD candidate from the school of Education, who is from Tanzania, and had participated in our seminar over the past three years, commented:

You guys should acknowledge the seminar in your proposals. We all have benefited greatly from the research seminars; from conceptualizing the research to the end of our thesis... it is of significant help indeed!

The research seminar has empowered students with academic abilities and skills that assist their research activities and provide new avenues of communication within educational fields through their increased familiarity of autonomous leadership and democratic participation, which in our view are essential qualities of academics. However, the variety of meanings of the intercultural collaborations and cooperation that occur throughout the seminars is significant, and goes beyond the more detailed elements of a conventional education program. Together with the autonomous and democratic participation experience, many students had the sense that it felt like a "mini UN conference" and they have expressed the view that they would take such a research seminar practice back to their home countries.

For example, the following from a PhD student from Ghana:

The fact that there is a seminar committee manned by students is a good thing that I hope to take back.

And further from a PhD student from Pakistan:

I will try to hold such [a] research seminar in my society. I will try to hold it regularly without credit hours.

CONCLUSION

My fundamental understanding is that the quality pursued in the research seminar of NU is fully within the spirit of the university and the aspirations of higher education, namely, to create an autonomous and democratic way of pursuing truth. This chapter was interpretive of that, based on the interview responses of participants who are key stakeholders in the English instruction program, and more importantly, where the supervised student autonomous research seminar is the key focus. It is both an exploratory as well as a descriptive write-up of a unique vision (the seminar) under this program in the faculty of education at NU in mainland China. The intention of this study is not necessarily to generalize this experience, though the seminar and the ideas generated from the study are worth spreading. Moreover, considering the growing interest and increasing number of international students with their range of diversity gained from studying in full English instruction programs in China, it is inevitable that Chinese universities need an innovative model in the pursuit for quality with academic autonomy in this cross-cultural learning environment. Consequently, the unique vision of a multidisciplinary and multicultural seminar focused on assisting students in actualizing their goals seems to be a problem-solving approach to the challenges in establishing a classroom culture that can promote the goals of the English instruction program and the designing of pedagogy that allows for a process of increasingly linguistic as well as a culture of effective group interaction.

Notably, the concept of quality in higher education is extremely abstract and individually based, since no single definition cuts across every aspect from the guidelines of the ministry, right down to the expectations of the academy and the students. Yet, in the faculty of education at NU, the English instruction program has managed to come up with a model, which, if paid more attention to, may actually be one of the unique answers to the multidisciplinary and multicultural nurturing of the next generation in the quest for the internationalization of higher education. From the interview responses, students emphasize the autonomy, diplomacy, as well as all-round academic and cross-cultural growth that they achieved through the seminar. In summary, this can be used as a somewhat clear symbol of the pursuit of quality by both international students and the faculty at the micro institutional level. This pursuit of quality at the micro level if encouraged and duplicated may have ripple effects at the macro levels.

NOTES

1. "Visiting scholars" are those making an academic stay in this program for one or two semesters but not for degrees. Most of them are Chinese government scholarship holders. Some of them were MA or PhD holders before they attended the program. All visiting scholars participate in all academic activities and are required to accomplish a research paper by the end of their visit or stay.
2. 99 percent of them had no Mandarin learning experience before coming to this program and their first language is not English.
3. The students have diverse academic backgrounds: including Adult Education, Applied Linguistics, Cognitive Psychology, Counseling Psychology, Early Childhood Education, Higher Education, and Education Management.
4. As the practice of most universities in the world nowadays, International Association of University also considers teaching, research, and service as three main components of the quality of higher education. (http://www.iau-aiu.net/, accessed June 3, 2016)
5. All the participant names used in this chapter are pseudonyms.
6. When this chapter was being prepared, Iren had accomplished her PhD thesis proposal rehearsal at the seminar, which is about Russian citizenship education.
7. To support mentorship constructing, the seminar has started a new content of discussant. The discussant is responsible to review the speaker's proposal or thesis rehearsal draft before seminar. After the presentation, the discussant would give comments and ask critical questions to initiate the seminar discussion.

REFERENCES

Hayhoe, R., & Liu, J. (2010). China's universities, cross-border education and the dialogue among civilizations. In D. W. Chapman, W. K. Cummings, & G. A. Postiglione (Eds.), *Border crossing in East Asian higher education* (pp. 77–100). Hong Kong: Comparative Education Research Centre and Springer.

Marshall, G. (1998). *Dictionary of sociology*. Oxford: Oxford University Press.

UNESCO. (2010). *Global education digest 2010: Comparing education statistics across the world* (p. 172). Montreal: UNESCO Institute for Statistics.

Zhu, H., & Ma, Y. P. (2011). 2011 New patterns in higher education cross-cultural learning: The case of a postgraduate English instruction program in China. *Frontier of Education China, 6*(4), 471–494.

STATISTICS ABOUT CHINESE INTERNATIONAL STUDENTS (SOURCES)

2011:   http://www.moe.gov.cn/publicfiles/business/htmlfiles/moe/s5147/201202/131263.html

2012: http://www.moe.gov.cn/publicfiles/business/htmlfiles/moe/moe_863/201303/148379.html

2013:   http://www.moe.gov.cn/publicfiles/business/htmlfiles/moe/s5987/201402/164235.html

2014:   http://www.moe.edu.cn/publicfiles/business/htmlfiles/moe/s5987/201503/184959.html

Ministry of Education of the People's Republic of China. (2011). Over 260 000: International students studying in China in 2010. Retrieved July 6, 2011, from http://www.moe.gov.cn/publicfiles/business/htmlfiles/moe/s3124/201002/82570.html

NENU. (2015). *International Student Office Archive*. Changchun: Northeast Normal University.

OECD. (2010). Education at a glance 2010: OECD indicators. Retrieved July 6, 2011, from http://www.oecd.org/document/52/0,3746,en_2649_39263238_45897844_1_1_1_1,00.ht

UNESCO. (2009). *Global education digest 2009: Comparing education statistics across the world*. Montreal: UNESCO Institute for Statistics.

UNESCO. (2010). *Global education digest 2010: Comparing education statistics across the world*. Montreal: UNESCO Institute for Statistics.

Zhejiang Provincial Education Association for International Students. (2009). A comprehensive review of the situation regarding international students in China. Retrieved July 6, 2011, from http://zeaie.zjedu.org/dtxx/2009-5/200483198909282870012043232176.html

Higher Education Massification and Quality Assurance in Vietnam: A Case Study of Viet Nam National University Ho Chi Minh City

Nguyen Thi Thanh Nhat and Pham Thi Bich

INTRODUCTION

During the last two decades, higher education has expanded around the world more than ever before. In line with the global trend, the massification process in Vietnam has proceeded rapidly as a result of an impressive economic growth and a culture that highly respects learning. However, besides these achievements, the rapid expansion of higher education has resulted in raising various issues, especially an increase in the existence of low-quality programs and a mismatch between industry requirements

N.T.T. Nhat (✉)
Center for Educational Testing and Quality Assessment, Viet Nam National University Ho Chi Minh City (VNU-HCM), Ho Chi Minh City, Vietnam

P.T. Bich
Center for Educational Testing and Quality Assessment, Viet Nam National University Ho Chi Minh City (VNU-HCM), Ho Chi Minh City, Vietnam

© The Author(s) 2017
D.E. Neubauer, C. Gomes (eds.),
Quality Assurance in Asia-Pacific Universities,
DOI 10.1007/978-3-319-46109-0_6

and the knowledge and skills possessed by university graduates. The Vietnamese government is well aware of the need to address the challenges brought by the massification process. One primary focus has been the establishment of a quality assurance (QA) mechanism. At present, the mechanism is relatively complete. However, strong emphasis is placed on a standard-based accreditation system while other more complex and sensitive QA elements have not yet been developed or implemented. In such a context, the extent to which a Vietnamese higher education institution (HEI) invests in internal quality assurance (IQA) could determine its place on the QA development map. This chapter provides an overview of the massification of Vietnam's higher education during the last two decades and efforts initiated by the government to develop a national QA system. It also presents the IQA system of Viet Nam National University Ho Chi Minh City (VNU-HCM) as a case study to demonstrate that within the context of Vietnamese Higher Education, the national framework for QA practice still needs time for improvement. As such, HEIs need to actively develop and improve their own IQA to catch up with regional and international developments.

MASSIFICATION IN VIETNAM'S HIGHER EDUCATION

In the last few decades, higher education has expanded around the world. In line with this global trend, the massification process in Vietnam has proceeded rapidly as a result of impressive economic growth and a culture that highly respects learning. During the period 1995 to 2012, the number of higher education students has dramatically increased from 354,103 to 2,177,299, while the number of universities and colleges has risen from 110 to 421.[1] Since 2000, much of the growth in the system has been in the form of new and expanding private sector institutions. Thang Long People-Founded University, the first nonpublic institution was established in 1988 served as a pilot project. Subsequently, the number of non-public HEIs in Vietnam grew impressively in number. By 2012, 54 universities and 29 colleges had been established, accounting for 19 percent of the total institutions and 14 percent of the total number of students in the HEI system.[2] Improving and widening domestic provision has been a recent priority of the Vietnamese government. Increasing the higher education participation rate is considered one of the key elements to achieve the development goal of becoming an industrialized economy by 2020. In its "Socio-Economic Development Plan 2006–2010", the government aimed to increase enrollment in universities and colleges by 10 percent annually. The goal was to reach a ratio of 200 students for every 10,000 people by 2010 and 450 students for every 10,000 people by 2020.[3]

However, the lack of strong management tools directed at improving academic and administrative quality has raised concerns about a possible overall deterioration of the system. In January 2014, the government halted enrollment in 207 undergraduate programs at 71 universities and colleges due to a lack of qualified teaching staff. In addition, the labor market is still in need of graduates with appropriate knowledge and skills, while the overall output of HEIs has outnumbered industry demand in terms of the number of graduates they produce. Many graduates experience difficulties in finding jobs, while others end up unemployed or underemployed (Tran 2010). Quality issues are among the key factors that have led to the increase in the number of Vietnamese students going abroad for higher education—termed "education refugees" by many domestic academics. According to the Ministry of Education and Training (MOET), the number of Vietnamese students pursuing studies overseas in 2013 reached 125,000, representing a 15 percent increase over 2012 and the largest year-over-year jump since 2008–2009 (ICEF 2014). It is widely acknowledged in Vietnamese academic community and among international observers that the system requires significant improvements in both the standard of its programs and the outcomes for graduates. As stated by a 2008 World Bank Report titled "Vietnam: Higher Education and Skills for Growth", "the fast growing Vietnamese economy and the increasing need for innovation and high quality skills is putting demands on a higher education system that is not yet fully equipped to respond" (World Bank 2008).

THE DEVELOPMENT OF QUALITY ASSURANCE IN VIETNAM

The Vietnamese government is well aware of the need to address the challenges brought by the massification process. Hence the setting up of a QA mechanism has been a top higher education priority. Compared with its development in many other global settings, quality assurance is relatively new to Vietnam. Modern QA was initially introduced into the country's higher education system via the World Bank's First Higher

Education Project in the late 1990s. This scheme provided some funding to the first institutional QA centers—the Center for Education Quality Assurance and Research Development (CEQARD) in Hanoi and the Center for Educational Testing and Quality Assessment (CETQA) in Ho Chi Minh City—established at two national universities (Viet Nam National University Ho Chi Minh City and Vietnam National University, Hanoi). Before that, no mechanisms for QA existed other than the original scrutiny required for approval of a new institution. All university operations were placed under the strong control of MOET, and its management was considered as a guarantor of quality (Sheridan 2010). With the expansion of the higher education system, the government has taken new steps to support an enhanced level of QA. In 2002, an accreditation unit was established inside the Department for Undergraduate Education (now the Department for Higher Education) of MOET. In 2003, the unit was separated from the Department of Undergraduate Education and was officially named the General Department for Educational Testing and Accreditation (GDETA). According to Decree 85/2003/NĐ-CP, GDETA operates directly under the supervision of MOET. GDETA acts as a national governmental agency to supervise all QA activities for the whole national education system; participating in the policymaking process including the development of quality standards. At the institutional level, with lessons learned from the first two QA centers at the two national universities, other HEIs in the country, mainly regional universities whose organizational structures are similar to the two national universities, also established their own QA units in the early 2000s. In late 2007, the establishment of a QA unit in the organizational structure of a university or college was a compulsory requirement of the quality standards for accreditation at institutional level promulgated by MOET.[4]

With the support of the World Bank (HEP1 Project) and the Dutch government (ProfQim Project), a standard-based accreditation system has also been developed. Based on the inputs of universities as well as from local and international experts, MOET formulated a set of ten quality standards and 53 criteria as the core of a provisional regulation for the accreditation of universities which was published in 2004.[5] The ministry also implemented an institutional accreditation pilot project for 20 universities in Vietnam. One of the outcomes of this pilot project was the revised set of ten standards issued by MOET in November 2007 as the regulations for accreditation of universities.[4] Also in November that year, the set of ten quality standards for accreditation of colleges was issued.[6] At the program level, it was not until March 2016 that a set of 11 criteria for higher education accreditation at the program level was issued by MOET via circular number 04/2016/TT-BGDĐT. The majority of these requirements are similar to the third version of the ASEAN (Association of Southeast Asian Nations) University Network-Quality Assurance (AUN-QA) criteria for quality assessment at the program level, which were issued by the AUN in 2015.[7] Further information about this organization will be presented later in this chapter. With such changes, accreditation was no longer regarded as a voluntary activity. In 2015, the results of higher education accreditation at both institutional and program levels were listed as one standard to stratify HEIs by the government in decree number 73/2015/NĐ-CP. To gain qualification through the standards set out by this decree, all HEIs must be accredited. In addition, during the past few years, four centers for education accreditation have been established, including the VNU Center of Education Accreditation (VNU-CEA) of VNU-Hanoi and the VNU-HCM Center of Education Accreditation (VNU-HCM-CEA) of VNU-HCM, the Center of Education Accreditation—The University of Danang, and the Center for Education Accreditation of Association of Vietnam Universities and Colleges (CEA-AVU&C). Up to April 2016, only the centers of the two national universities have implemented accreditation activities, which are limited to the institutional level. No educational programs have been accredited by domestic accreditation agencies at that point.

Today the national QA framework in Vietnam can be seen as somewhat complete with internal QA units within all HEIs, and the establishment of external QA agencies and external QA standards & processes. However, the system is far from being perfect. Several issues remain that need to be addressed so that the mechanism can bring about positive impacts on the quality of higher education. These considerations include the following:

1. Three of the four centers for education accreditation are under the direct supervision of public universities funded by the government. This has raised concerns for the independence status of these external QA agencies.
2. The standard-based accreditation system does not promote diversification of HEIs, a consideration that many hold to be very much necessary for Vietnam's higher education system. It is worth noting

that the higher education system in Vietnam is very complex with its combination of national and regional universities, research institutes, academies, comprehensive universities, specialized universities, technical and vocational colleges, teacher training colleges, community colleges and professional secondary schools.

3. At present, the national QA framework relies only on a basic system of accreditation. It is highly desirable that other elements be included to stimulate a quality culture. The implementation of IQA within HEIs has resulted from the need to meet the requirements by MOET rather than the inner drive for continuous improvement.

4. In the presentation titled "Higher Education Quality Assurance in Vietnam and Improvement for Better Collaboration", Pham XuanThanh, former general deputy director of GDETA pointed out that QA at the program level is not well developed (Thanh, P. X. 2013).

5. There remains a serious lack of QA experts in higher education.

As a result of all these factors, the impacts on the quality of higher education teaching and learning of QA are still limited and vary from institution to institution. In such a context, the emphasis on IQA of each HEI plays a decisive role in pushing the institutions beyond the minimum standards. The following sections present the IQA system of VNU-HCM as a typical case study of such efforts.

IQA System of Viet Nam National University Ho Chi Minh City

Background

VNU-HCM was established in January 1995 as a national multidisciplinary university, formed by the merger of various prestigious universities in Ho Chi Minh City. VNU-HCM is currently comprised of six member universities, one research institute, one school and a number of affiliated centers and units. The member universities and research institute include the University of Technology, the University of Science, the University of Social Science and Humanities, the International University, the University of Information and Technology, the University of Economics and Law and the Institute for Environment and Resources. VNU-HCM's structure is presented in Fig. 6.1.

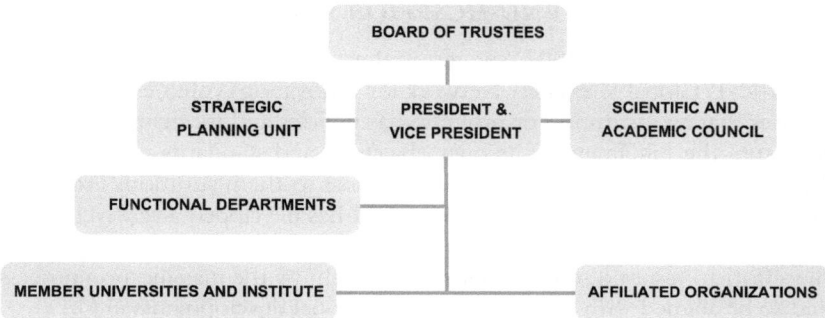

Fig. 6.1 VNU-HCM's organizational structure

With a total of **5662** faculty members, admin staff members and researchers, the university now provides graduate and postgraduate education to over **60,000** students, including[8]:

- 114 undergraduate programs
- 114 master's programs
- 84 doctoral programs

VNU-HCM is one of the two national universities in Vietnam (the other is Vietnam National University, Hanoi—VNU-Hanoi). Under government decree no. 186/2013/NĐ-CP, these universities enjoy special privileges. Their rectors are also appointed by the prime minister. In comparison to other public sector HEIs in the system, these two universities are also different, in that they have more academic and financial autonomy. For example, they have more freedom concerning budgetary decisions where they do not need to refer to the ministry for approval (Sheridan 2010). They also have the freedom to develop educational programs that are not included in the MOET-approved directory. In addition, as mentioned above, VNU-HCM and VNU-Hanoi are the first institutions to establish their own QA units, even before the establishment of GDETA, to test whether a QA mechanism would work in Vietnam. Without a national regulatory framework for QA practices by the time it was established, VNU-HCM learned from international and regional experience, especially AUN, to develop its own IQA system.

VNU-HCM's IQA System

As Sanyal and Martin (2007) suggest in their definitive chapter on quality in the GUNI (Global University Network for Innovation) volume on QA, IQA ensures that an institution or program has policies and mechanisms in place to ensure the fulfillment of its own objectives and standards while external QA is performed by an organization external to the institution. From this perspective, it can be said that VNU-HCM has developed a relatively complete IQA system. The IQA system may be seen as the outcome of a collective effort to respond to the challenges brought by the massification process and to be aligned with international and regional developments in QA.

VNU-HCM's QA unit was founded in 1999. Since then, other components of the IQA system have been gradually established. As an umbrella organization of six member universities, VNU-HCM chose to develop an IQA system based on a studied balance between centralization and decentralization. It consists of three levels: the overarching VNU-HCM level with a QA council and CETQA, followed by the institutional and faculty levels. This structure makes it possible for leadership guidance to be exercised through all levels while allowing for the active participation of member institutions. Functions and responsibilities of the system's individual components are clearly specified. Figure 6.2 shows how VNU's IQA system is structured.

At the top of the system, the QA council sets the direction and strategy for QA practice for the whole system. The QA units of the member universities develop their strategies in alignment with the VNU council and their own context. CETQA is a standing unit of VNU-HCM, playing the main role in coordinating, promoting and monitoring QA activities among member institutions. CETQA is under the direct guidance of the QA Council and vertically related to the other units of VNU-HCM's QA system. It is to some extent the bridge between the QA council and the QA units at the institutional level. The center plays double roles in the QA practice within the system: on the one hand, it performs IQA functions by supporting the member universities to improve their QA activities and organizing workshops for QA officers of these institutions, and on the other, it acts as an external agency to conduct site visits and the evaluation of member universities at both institutional and program levels.

In addition, the QA units at the institutional and faculty levels are in place at all VNU-HCM's member universities. These units directly implement QA activities, including QA planning, QA staff development, curriculum design and improvement, conducting surveys, collecting

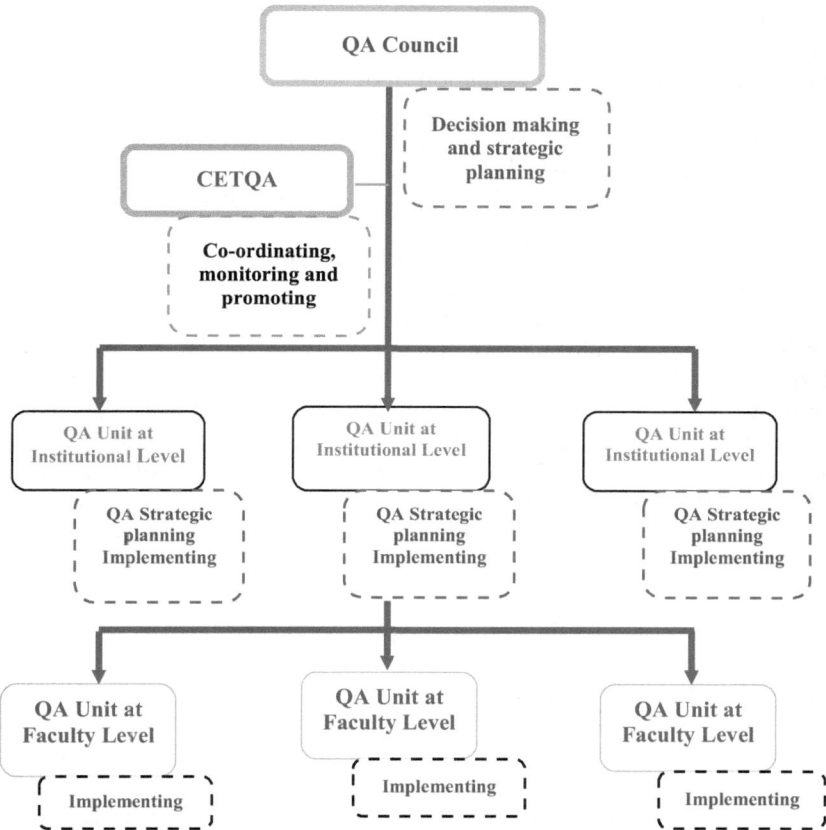

Fig. 6.2 VNU-HCM's IQA system

feedback from stakeholders and development of QA procedures. Based on the typical characteristics of individual institutions, each unit will develop its own way to effectively run the QA system with the ultimate goal of enhancing educational quality.

Quality Policy of VNU-HCM

The VNU-HCM's complex structure of multiple member universities and over **5000** staff complicates internal quality discussions. For this reason, if no other, when making reference to quality in this structure, it is important to speak the same language. Having a shared idea about quality is critical. Therefore, to promote a common understanding, VNU-HCM has adopted the following definition of quality:

> Quality is achieving our goals and aims in an efficient and effective way, assuming that the goals and aims reflect the requirements of all our stakeholders in an adequate way. (VNU-HCM's Quality Handbook 2015)

From this reference point, each member university can build its own operational definition of quality and strategy for QA. With the goal of becoming one of the top Asian higher education systems and a hub for scientific, technological and cultural development in its home country, during the last decade, VNU-HCM has placed emphasis on QA to continuously improve its training toward regional and international standards and to promote a consistent understanding of quality. In VNU-HCM's strategy for the periods of 2011–2015 and 2016–2020, QA is one of its top concerns. At the VNU-HCM level, the QA policy statement for the entire VNU-HCM system maintains the following principles and practices:

1. Quality is the top priority in VNU-HCM's development plan.
2. Quality must be thoroughly integrated in every activity of affiliated members.
3. Quality is diversity and autonomy—acknowledging the diversity among VNU-HCM's members. Open for assessment from different international and regional organizations such as AUN, ABET, et cetera.
4. Quality is continuous improvement—encouraging initiatives on increasing quality within VNU-HCM's systems and organizational structures.
5. Emphasis is placed first on QA activities, which must be implemented effectively and synchronously before engaging in accreditation and ranking.
6. Quality must be bottom up—prioritizing assessments at the program level.

(VNU-HCM's Quality Handbook 2015)

Based on these quality policies, VNU-HCM has developed the orientation for the system's QA practice as featured in Fig. 6.3.

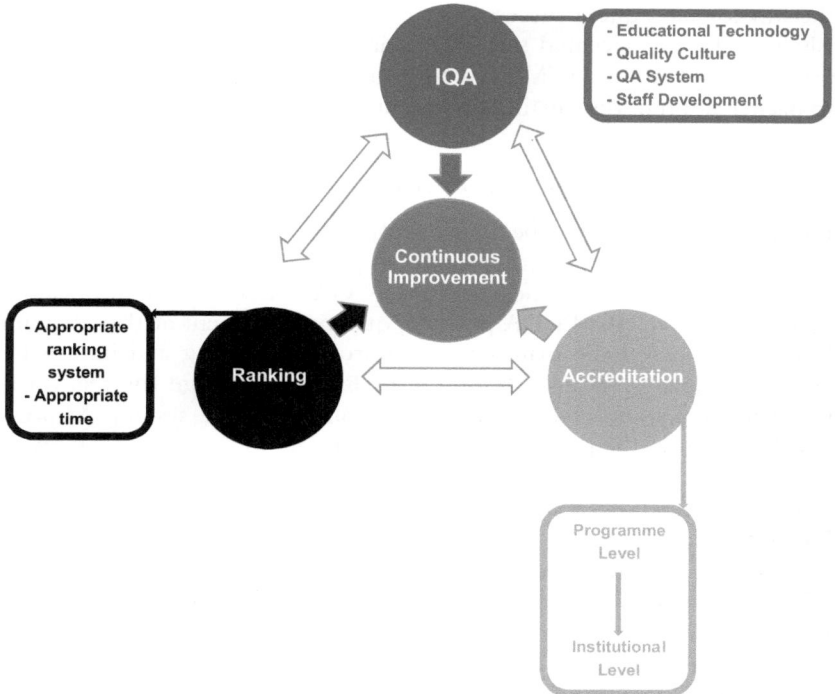

Fig. 6.3 Orientation for QA practice at VNU-HCM (adapted from the presentation titled "Quality Assurance at Viet Nam National University Ho Chi Minh City: Development and Integration" of Nguyen Hoi Nghia—Vice President of VNU-HCM at the workshop held by VNU-HCM on "Quality Assurance and Accreditation in higher education: ways toward international integration" on November 13, 2014) (Nghia, N. H. 2014)

As indicated from these policies, VNU-HCM has placed emphasis on educational technology and QA as a starting point before participating in accreditation and then joining the ranking process. Promoting innovation in educational technology through curriculum design, teaching and learning methods and so on, is an effective way to achieve the objective of providing high quality human resources to meet increasingly high demands of the globalized community.

Furthermore, a dominant premise is that effective implementation of QA activities will lay the foundation for continuous improvement, paving the way for subsequent successful quality assessment according to regionally and globally accepted sets of criteria. Following accreditation at the program level, VNU-HCM moved on to institutional accreditation prior to participation in the ranking process at an appropriate time.

Internal Quality Assessment at Program Level

From the university's perspective, quality assessment "embraces all methods used to judge the performance of QA practices and activities at institutional, system or programme level" (AUN-QA assessor training workshop, 2013). In VNU-HCM's QA practice, quality assessment at the program level is considered the main driver towards maintaining and improving education quality because this is the best way to engage the real quality of members and create more impact on the whole system. At present, focusing on the program level is appropriate for resource mobility at VNU-HCM. Internal assessment activities are annually organized in all VNU-HCM member units. They are also the foundations for consolidating and developing VNU-HCM's quality culture.

With the support and approval from AUN, VNU-HCM is using AUN-QA criteria in its quality assessment at the program level. AUN was founded in 1995 and consists of leading universities in the region. Its main objective is to encourage and promote higher education cooperation and development in order to enhance regional integration in achieving global standards (ASEAN University Network 2016a). The initiative of quality assessment in accordance with AUN-QA was undertaken in 1998 in order to strengthen and sustain QA practices in ASEAN universities (ASEAN University Network 2011). The AUN-QA model was chosen as it was appropriate for the system for a number of reasons, including:

1. The AUN-QA set of criteria, tailor-designed for ASEAN higher education, is non-prescriptive and therefore could be used to assess the quality of programs of various fields. This is appropriate for quality assessment at VNU-HCM given that it is a multidisciplinary university.
2. The AUN-QA model for Program Level—3rd Version (as featured in Fig. 6.4) places emphasis on stakeholder needs and satisfaction which is aligned with regional and international trends. In an increasingly globalized world, HEIs are no longer ivory towers. From 2007 to 2013, every educational program offered by Vietnamese HEIs has

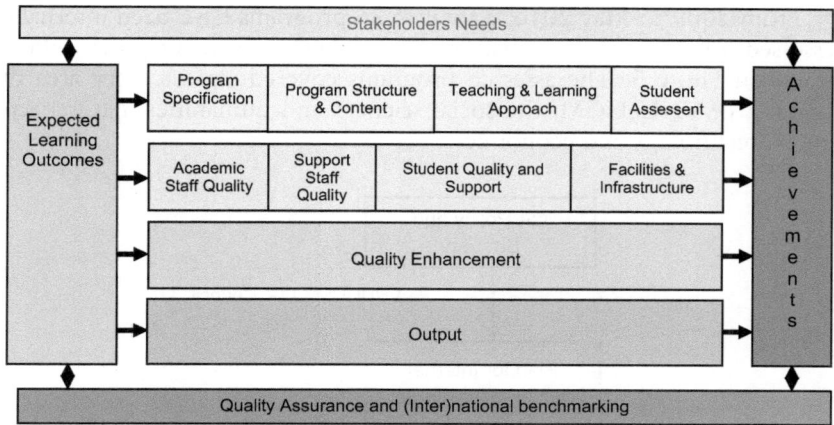

Fig. 6.4 AUN-QA model for program level—3rd version (adapted from guide to AUN-QA assessment at program level version 3.0)

had to follow the curriculum framework issued by the MOET. By the beginning of the year 2013, under Circular No 57/2012/TT-BGDĐT, the rector has the right to issue the curricula of the HEIs within his charge. This means that Vietnamese HEIs no longer needed to follow the MOET's curriculum framework and could from this point decide on their own curricula. As mentioned in the first part of this chapter, the rapid expansion of Vietnamese higher education system within a short period has resulted in various troublesome issues, especially the rapid increase in low-quality educational programs and the mismatch between industry requirements and the knowledge and skills of university graduates. Employing the framework of the AUN-QA model, VNU-HCM's member institutions are encouraged to take into consideration stakeholder needs to develop and assure the quality of the curriculum.

The AUN-QA model has become increasingly popular in the region. From 2007 to 2015, it has been utilized in more than 161 undergraduate and graduate programs in 27 Universities in 8 ASEAN countries and Timor-Leste (Document presented to AUN-QA Chief Quality Officers' Meeting, 2016b). Therefore, the use of AUN-QA criteria for internal quality assessment could facilitate increased regional integration and the preparation of programs for external quality assessment by AUN.

From 2009 to May 2016, a total of 36 programs have been internally assessed following the internal program quality assessment process illustrated in Fig. 6.5. The assessed programs covered almost every area of training of VNU-HCM: the social sciences and humanities, natural sciences, technology and economics.

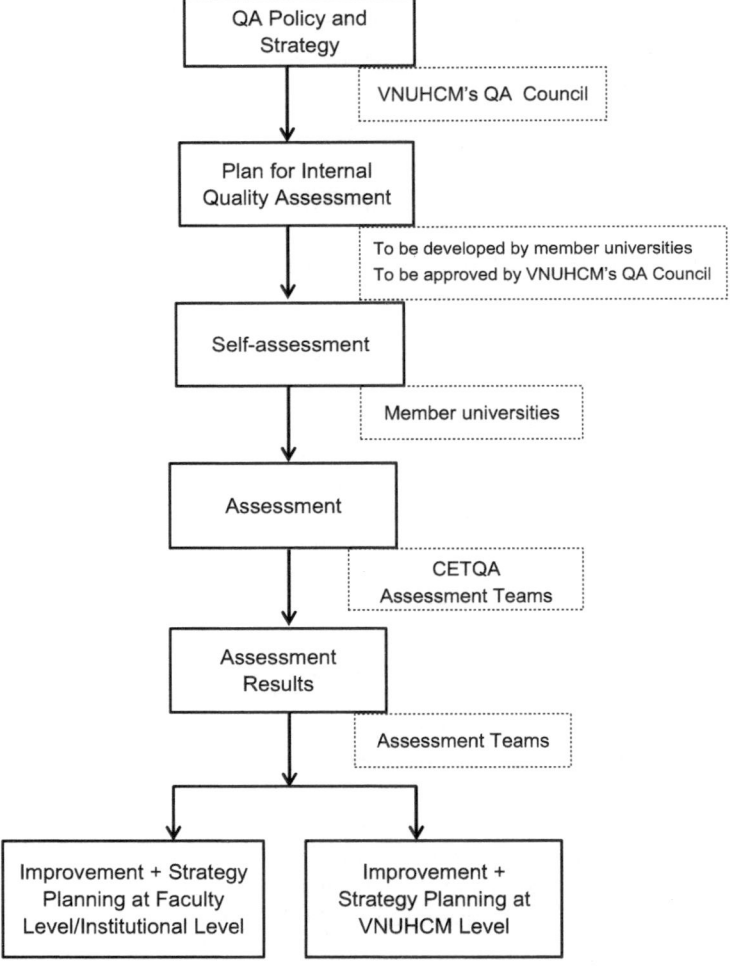

Fig. 6.5 Internal programmatic quality assessment process of VNU-HCM

Based on the QA policy and strategy issued by VNU-HCM's QA council, member universities will develop their plan for internal quality assessment, which nominates the specific programs to be assessed. Those programs that have been approved by the QA council will then prepare a self-assessment report. CETQA is in charge of the organization of internal assessments, including the setting up of assessment teams. These will work according to an assessment process similar to those developed by independent accreditation agencies. This arrangement is possible because the assessment team will not include lecturers or staff from the host universities. The activity creates a balanced combination of "internal" and "external" engagement as assessors come from VNU-HCM's member universities and other prestigious Vietnamese HEIs. At present, 48 lecturers and staff of VNU-HCM have attended AUN-QA program assessor training workshops. The number of assessors will increase in the next few years to accommodate the requirements of this activity as VNU-HCM is developing a plan to expand and upgrade its assessor network. Assessment results are submitted to CETQA, and the center subsequently reports to the QA council and member institutions. The results are used to develop improvement plans at VNU-HCM institutional and departmental levels. In addition, the good practices revealed through this process will be shared among VNU-HCM's member universities.

Through the years, internal quality assessment at the program level has proven to be an effective way to monitor and improve education quality, promote innovation in teaching and learning, and bring quality awareness to lecturers and support staff. The impact is not limited to some elements of universities (department or faculty) but has extended throughout the whole institution, drawing the active participation of stakeholders such as faculty, support staff, students, alumni and employers. The activity also helps strengthen the link between QA units at the VNU-HCM level and those at an institutional level, gradually building up a quality culture within the system.

Program internal quality assessment has also helped the institutions to prepare for external quality assessment. Up to January 2016, a total of 23 educational programs offered by VNU-HCM's member universities had successfully undergone AUN-QA quality assessment and achieved AUN-QA quality certificates. The assessment scores have significantly increased during the last few years. In 2015, two programs from the International University achieved scores of 5.0/7 and 5.1/7 for

AUN-QA quality assessment (in the fields of the Bachelor of Engineering in Biomedical Engineering and Bachelor of Engineering in Industrial & Systems Engineering)—the second highest scores in the region. In addition, in 2014, the University of Technology became the first Vietnamese HEI to achieve ABET accreditation in two majors: computer science and computer engineering. Many degrees awarded by VNU-HCM's member universities are recognized beyond Vietnam in the USA, Australia, Asian or European countries, paving the way for higher instances of regional and internal integration.

However, besides these achievements, QA practice at VNU-HCM still faces many challenges, including:

- the lack of QA experts and quality innovations;
- the resistance of a number of lecturers and staff to the process because it is financially and time-consuming;
- the uneven development in QA practices among member universities;
- because of globalization, higher education keeps changing, and as a result, it is not easy to attune the QA system to external developments.

These challenges could slow down the progress of quality assurance if timely solutions are not found.

CONCLUSION

The rapid expansion of Vietnamese higher education presented new challenges for the government as well as for HEIs in assuring and improving overall quality. During the last two decades, a national QA mechanism has emerged in Vietnam and a standard-based accreditation system has developed. However, there is still much to be done before the significance on the overall patterns and processes of higher education quality can be quantified. Since it takes time and resources to improve the QA system at the national level, it has been necessary for HEIs to focus on their own IQA practices in response to the challenges presented both by globalization and the attendant processes of massification. HEIs are no longer ivory towers. The level of expectation that stakeholders, including students and industry, have in terms of the demand they place on education service providers has also elevated. The efforts made by VNU-HCM can serve as a good example of how a Vietnamese HEIs may respond to similar challenges.

NOTES

1. The data are sourced from MOET at different times. The 1995 data is extracted from World Bank Country Study: Vietnam-Education Financing, which was published in 1997 (Table 2.5) and is accessible at http://www-wds.worldbank.org/external/default/WDS ContentServer/WDSP/IB/1997/09/01/000009265_39711131 51139/Rendered/PDF/multi_page.pdf, accessed on June 2, 2016. The 2012 data is extracted from the statistics provided on the website of MOET, which is accessible at http://www.moet.gov.vn/?page=11.11&view=5251, accessed on June 2, 2016
2. Source: MOET. Accessible at http://www.moet.gov.vn/?page=11.11&view=5251, accessed on June 2, 2016
3. Socio-Economic Development Plan 2006–2010, attachment to Government Resolution No. 25/2006/NQ-CP, dated October 9, 2006.
4. Decision number 65/2007/QĐ-BGDĐT dated November 01, 2007, on the promulgation of the Regulation on Quality Standards for accreditation of universities.
5. Decision number 38/2004/QĐ-BGDĐT dated December 02, 2004, on the promulgation of the provisional Regulation on the accreditation of universities.
6. Decision number 66/2007/QĐ-BGDĐT dated November 01, 2007, on the promulgation of the Regulation on Quality Standards for accreditation of colleges.
7. Guide to AUN-QA Assessment at Program Level, version 3.0.
8. Source: VNUHCM's Prospectus.

REFERENCES

ASEAN University Network. (2011). *Guide to AUN actual quality assessment at programme level*. Accessible at http://www.aunsec.org/pdf/documentations/02_GuidetoAUNActualQualityAssessmentatProgrammeLevel-15Criteria.pdf. Accessed 20 May 2016.

ASEAN University Network. (2013). *The document of AUN-QA assessor training workshop*.

ASEAN University Network. (2015). *Guide to AUN-QA assessment at programme level, version 3.0*. Accessible at http://www.aunsec.org/pdf/Guide%20to%20AUN-QA%20Assessment%20at%20Programme%20Level%20Version%203_2015.pdf. Accessed 20 May 2016.

ASEAN University Network. (2016a). *Official website.* Accessible at http://www. aunsec.org/. Accessed 20 May 2016.

ASEAN University Network. (2016b). *Document for AUN-QA Chief Quality Officers' Meeting in 2016.*

ICEF Monitor. (2014). *Number of Vietnamese students abroad up 15 % in 2013.* Accessible at http://monitor.icef.com/2014/11/number-vietnamese-students-abroad-15-2013/. Accessed 20 May 2016.

Nghia, N. H. (2014). *Quality assurance at Viet Nam National University Ho Chi Minh City: Development and integration.* Presentation presented at the workshop held by VNUHCM on "Quality Assurance and Accreditation in higher education: ways towards international integration" on November 13, 2014.

Sanyal, B. C., & Martin, M. (2007). *Quality assurance and the role of accreditation: An overview.* Report: Higher Education in the World 2007: Accreditation for quality assurance: What is at stake?

Sheridan, G. (2010). *Consultant report: Vietnam higher education sector analysis.* Accessible at http://www.adb.org/sites/default/files/project-document/63092/42079-01-vie-tacr-03.pdf. Accessed 15 May 2016.

Thanh, P. X. (2013). *Higher education quality assurance in Vietnam and improvement for better collaboration.* Presentation presented at the event under the theme: "Connecting Asia—preparing higher education to meet the demand of the 21st century" held by British Council in Vietnam as part of Global Education Dialogues: The East Asia series. Accessible at https://www.british-council.vn/sites/default/files/ged_2013_day_1_group_2_dr_pham_xuan_thanh.pdf. Accessed 16 May 2016.

Tran, T. T. (2010). *Enhancing graduate employability: Challenges facing higher education in Vietnam.* Paper presented at the 14th UNESCO-APEID International Conference: Education for Human Resource Development, Bangkok, Thailand.

VNU-HCM. (2015). *VNUHCM's quality handbook.*

VNUHCM's Prospectus, 2015.

VNU-HCM's Strategic Plan for quality assurance period 2011–2015; period 2016–2020.

World Bank. (1997). *Vietnam – Education financing. A World Bank country study.* Washington, DC: The World Bank.

World Bank. (2008). *Report titled "Vietnam: Higher Education and Skills for Growth".* Accessible at http://siteresources.worldbank.org/INTEASTASIAPACIFIC/Resources/Vietnam-HEandSkillsforGrowth.pdf. Accessed 10 May 2016.

CHAPTER 7

Quality Assurance in the Era of Mass Higher Education in Japan

Shangbo Li

INTRODUCTION

The concept of "quality assurance" has been the focus of much attention in the era of mass higher education in Japan. Many symposia and conferences have been devoted to education quality and hosted by relevant stakeholders in government and in universities. Most of these events have been concerned with various issues surrounding accreditation and assessment activities as performed by external agencies and in alignment with the policies of the Ministry of Education, Culture, Sports, Science and Technology (MEXT). MEXT is particularly important because universities in Japan are quite diverse, united only by MEXT's jurisdiction over them.

Using J. F. Oberlin University as a specific example, this chapter, therefore, (1) focuses on the general question of "how is quality generated and maintained at the institutional level?" It then (2) explores the implications of practices of the university to clarify the particular range of elements that have emerged within today's institutional context, and the particular ways

S. Li (✉)
Institute of Education Research, The Open University of China,
Beijing, China

© The Author(s) 2017
D.E. Neubauer, C. Gomes (eds.),
Quality Assurance in Asia-Pacific Universities,
DOI 10.1007/978-3-319-46109-0_7

in which this university has been affected by events within more macro contextual levels. Sources used include Japanese government documents, data from J. F. Oberlin University and the results of previous research in the area of quality education.

WHO ARE THE EVALUATION BODIES?

The environment surrounding higher education in Japan has changed considerably. Since 2004, all universities, junior colleges and colleges of technology are obliged to undergo review by an evaluation organization certified by MEXT. The purpose of the evaluation is to ensure the quality of higher education institutions (HEIs). Universities are open to receive the more general evaluations of society after the evaluation results are published, implemented, and then plan for self-improvement based on the evaluation results.

Currently, the quality assurance bodies in charge of universities are the Japan University Accreditation Association (JUAA), the National Institution for Academic Degrees and Quality Enhancement of Higher Education (NIAD-QE) and the Japan Institution for Higher Education Evaluation (JIHEE).

JUAA was established in 1947 under the sponsorship of 46 national, local public and private universities.[1] It was recognized by MEXT as the first Certified Evaluation and Accreditation Agency for universities on August 31, 2004. JUAA currently covers 340 member universities, including 20 national universities, 46 local public universities and 274 private universities. NIAD-QE's predecessor was the NIAD founded in 1991. In 2004, the NIAD-UE was newly established in accordance with the Act on General Rules for Independent Administrative Agency and the Act on the NIAD-UE an Independent Administrative Agency. In January 2005, NIAD-UE was certified by MEXT as an evaluation and accreditation organization for universities. It publicly announced the results of its evaluation of teaching and research activities at national university corporations for the first time in 2009. In 2016, NIAD-QE was established by the merger of NIAD-UE and the Center for National University Finance and Management (CUFM).

In a separate set of decisions, a resolution to establish a third-party institution for the evaluation of private universities was adopted at the 117th general meeting of the Association of Private Universities of Japan (APUJ) in October 2002.[2] APUJ's view was that a flexible and more elastic evaluation system could better correspond to the scale and diversity of private universities, a decision that resulted from an extensive study of the existing higher education evaluation system in Japan. The establishment of JIHEE was authorized by MEXT in November 2004. The objectives of JIHEE are to evaluate how educational and research activities are conducted at private universities and to assist in their self-initiated endeavors to enhance and improve the quality of higher education. With that mission, its focus is to actively contribute to the overall development of the 340 private universities in Japan. In summary, the ultimate objective of these three agencies is to contribute to the development of higher education by carrying out evaluation duties across a complex set of institutions that differ in important respects.

How Is Quality Generated at the Institutional Level?

Japan has the most mature higher education system in East Asia (Umagoshi 2004). However, as indicated, formal governmental quality assurance at the institutional level has existed for just over a decade. The introduction of a quality assurance system within the government was first reflected in a report by the Central Council for Education (CCE).

On August 5, 2002, the CCE, the most important council within MEXT, released "A Report on Building of a New System Which Affects the Quality Assurance of universities," which emphasized the necessity of creating an overall system of university quality assurance (CCE 2002). As of October 2001, 92 percent of Japanese universities, including national universities, local public and private universities, were conducting some form of self-assessment, with 75 percent publishing what they deemed relevant results, but with only 32 percent of these universities utilizing some form of third-party review. The problems as indicated by the report lay in the fact that almost all self-checking and self-evaluations of quality were conducted and evaluated by the universities themselves. The prevailing view was that it was difficult to ensure public transparency and objectivity of such a process and its subsequent evaluations.

The report cites both international and domestic reasons for introducing some form of a third-party evaluation system nationwide. The international factor lay in the reality that developed countries regard university quality evaluation as an important higher education issue. Throughout the 1980s and 1990s, overall emphasis on higher education quality assurance systems was introduced and given stronger emphasis due to the extraordinary expansion and massification of higher education during these decades. References to such developments in the USA, the UK, France and Germany were increasingly common. Therefore, in the opinion of the CCE, it was necessary to build a quality assurance system that would guarantee education and research quality in Japanese society on a constant basis, in order to ensure the international universality of the level of education and research. The CCE emphasized the possibility of generating changes in the approval system for the establishment of universities. Deregulation and the granting of more flexibility in the establishment of universities were discussed as a major development advantage by the report. In fact, substantial reforms aimed at deregulation and providing for more flexibility in the establishment of new universities were initiated in April 2003.[3] The government intended to establish a general evaluation system for both domestic and international situations as well. As indicated above, a formal evaluation system for universities in Japan was initiated on April 1, 2004 (Tachi 2007). Universities in Japan were thereafter obligated to periodically undergo third-party evaluation.

The root cause of these reforms is the combination of a quantitative expansion of Japanese higher education and the country's declining birthrate. In Japan, the total fertility rates (TFR)—the average number of children a woman bears over her lifetime—bottomed out at 1.26 births per woman in 2005. While "the TFR has been slowly but steadily growing, ... the government is predicting a 0.01-point dip— for 2015."[4] Furthermore, on January 28, 2005, CCE released a report entitled "The Future of Higher Education in Japan," which focused on the new trends in quantitative changes to higher education, and forecasted that the capacity of HEIs would soon reach their saturation point, since the ratio of enrollees to the number of applicants at universities and junior colleges would reach 100 percent by 2007. Therefore, the important issue in the future, stressed by the report, would be the consequent development of higher education in a situation in which anyone can undertake study in the field of their choice and at any time (MEXT 2005).

In retrospect, it can be said that the massification of higher education, combined with a declining birthrate, and the capacity of the system of higher education to satisfy all potential demand have contributed the basic impetus for quality assurance to become a significant issue in Japanese higher education.

Defining Criteria

Along with the massification of higher education and its impact on several areas of development, how to protect learners and maintain international validity with respect to perceptions of higher education quality emerged as a significant issue. Finding ways to articulate, measure and assess the criteria associated with providing accurate oversight of quality, therefore, have become a priority for the government.

All of the evaluation criteria with regard to university establishment standards of quality were based on the Ministry of Education's 28th order of 1956. However on July 31, 2007, MEXT issued "The Enforcement such as Departmental Orders to Revise a Part of the University Setting Standards" (Notice) which took effect on April 1, 2008. This notice was based on the previously adopted 2005 policy report "The Future of Higher Education in Japan," and defined measures held necessary to improve educational quality across academic departments as well as the standards that universities should meet in order to clearly guarantee the quality of their education.

The 2007 notice mandates a range of standards and outcomes that all universities must meet, including the following that have specifically related to education at J. F. Oberlin (MEXT 2009): (1) an objective clarification of fields of study, (2) the necessity to make a formal request if professors and facilities are to be distributed across two or more campuses, (3) the formal establishment of class subjects, (4) calculation standards for issuing credits based on two or more methods, (5) clearly stated standards for student evaluation, (6) organized training for faculty development, (7) admission of auditors and other special students, (8) exclusive use of facilities and so on.

Fundamentally, the aforementioned evaluation bodies are charged with performing a comprehensive review of a university's teaching and research on campuses at least once every seven years based on these new standards. Moreover, universities with professional graduate schools will also have their curriculum, faculty organization, and other general education and research situations reviewed at least once every five years based on the 2007 criteria.

The Practices at J. F. Oberlin

In Japan, it is expected that all universities will make continuous efforts to assure and improve their quality of education and research. For Japanese HEIs, the existing external quality assurance framework consists of the

Quality Assurance and Accreditation System (QAAS), the Standards for Establishing University (SEU) and the establishment-approval system (EAS).

QAAS is a mandatory evaluation for all universities reviewing their overall conditions of education and research. This scheme is conducted by the aforementioned three evaluation bodies.[5] Subject universities can select one or two certified organizations. In general, national university corporations follow the requirements of MEXT and choose NIAD-QE.

The SEU states the basic requirements for establishing a new university. It also functions as a minimum quality standard that existing universities must maintain. SEU covers education and research structures, curricula, academic staff and facilities. The standards are stipulated by the type of institution and school. Universities are responsible for meeting these requirements.

EAS is a systematic process for approving the establishment of a university. MEXT asks the Council for University Chartering and School Corporation to examine applications. The minister subsequently makes a final decision on approval. The council consists of two subcommittees: one focuses on university chartering by examining aspects of teaching and learning,[6] and the other thoroughly examines the process in accordance with relevant regulations, including the standards for the establishment of universities.

Although the threefold quality assurance framework described above exists throughout Japan, the faculty and students of J. F. Oberlin can only participate directly or realize matters organized by QAAS. The other two frameworks of quality assurance, those of the SEU, and the EAS, provide a structure that provides a template of prior regulatory measures for quality assurance. This allows the criteria to be known and made available in advance for use. In the EAS, for example, the head of a university such as the chancellor or president at J. F. Oberlin, will on occasion find it necessary to directly engage with this process and its requirements. For instance, J. F. Oberlin planned to build a new college of global communication in April 2016. Prior to this event, faculty and staff needed to support the chancellor in the process of planning and obtaining a setup permission from EAS. That said, most faculty members are not directly involved in this largely administratively directed process. SEU, on the other hand, will be concerned solely with those organizations that intend to establish a new university.

For most faculty members, quality assurance is most directly connected with their teaching and research roles. Teaching staff[7] are required to prepare complete syllabi for all courses they coordinate at the beginning of a new semester. Here they clearly identify the purpose of the course, provide a detailed schedule of specific methods of extracurricular study appropriate to the course, identify and make clear the marking and evaluation standard and provide information for office hours[8]. In addition, they also specify the appropriate contact method, including providing the office number, phone number and e-mail address. Every professor is required to be in his/her office during their office hours. Moreover, a professor must conduct 15 class sessions each semester in order to guarantee that students will have received the required time deemed appropriate for learning. If a lecture is canceled for some reason, a makeup session is required in all cases. At the end of the semester, student evaluations are conducted for each course. Every professor needs to provide his/her own comments about the results of student evaluation questionnaires and submit that review to his/her research unit head (*gakkeichō*). The research unit head must also provide feedback to the faculty member after reading the student questionnaires and the faculty member's comments.

Around the start of the academic year, all teaching staff must also submit a statement of objectives for the coming year and a self-evaluation for the past year. They will also receive feedback for these submissions from the head of their research unit. A Faculty Development (FD) Committee also convenes FD workshops at this time. J. F. Oberlin also supports a Faculty Development Center, concerned with both FD and the broader issue and process of staff development (SD). The center publishes its annual reports in March every year. For instance it described monthly meetings relating to FD and SD held in 2015 and the three symposia on higher educational issues it hosted in 2014 (J.F. Oberlin Faculty Development Center 2015). The center's annual report also contains details of monthly meetings related to institutional research (IR). Results of IR are published in J. F. Oberlin University's annual *Fact Book*, which is available to all stakeholders of J. F. Oberlin.

Activities related to quality assurance also take place within the framework of the school regulations (*gakusoku*) of J. F. Oberlin University. It can be said that the threefold quality assurance framework comprised of SEU, EAS and QAAS is working to provide an effective and efficient means for quality assurance at J. F. Oberlin University. This is borne out by the positive results of the evaluations by JIHEE in 2006 and 2012 and by JUAA in 2013.

IMPLICATIONS FOR PRACTICE

As mentioned above, an overall evaluation system for universities in Japan was created on April 1, 2004, and strict implementation began in 2008. J. F. Oberlin University is one of the institutions that has been evaluated under this system. Within this process and context, it is useful to inquire how these formal, external processes affect how quality is perceived and sought after for the daily operations of the university. In other words, to what extent have these external requirements operated to create a culture of quality within the university?

The education philosophy of J. F. Oberlin emphasizes the cultivation of truly globalized individuals. To succeed as such a person requires having the ability to employ reliable knowledge and skills. To nurture these skills, adequate provision can the inculcation of such outcomes in the classroom needs to be encouraged. Without this assurance, it is impossible to discuss matters of substance concerning students' potential and abilities. Indeed, a commonly cited perception within the country is that many Japanese students cannot explain aspects of their own country while overseas. Inadequate foreign language ability is one part of the problems. The language training resources at an internationalized campus like J. F. Oberlin, provides a means for addressing this issue.

As stated at the beginning of this chapter, the original motivation for quality assurance at the institutional level in Japanese higher education is to prevent a drop in quality resulting from the quantitative expansion of HEIs. As of August 7, 2014, the rate of college attendance in the country was 51.1 percent of the eligible age cohort. Enrolment in universities peaked in 2011 but witnessed decreases in each of the three consecutive years thereafter (MEXT 2014a) resulting in a significant system level overcapacity of available places for students. Virtually all universities, including J. F. Oberlin, are therefore confronting a management crisis brought about by this combination of massification and the shrinking college age cohort resulting from the declining birthrate. Amid this situation in which the very issue of continued fiscal viability for private HEIs is being called into question, in addition to the evaluation by JUAA cited above, J. F. Oberlin University has received an "A" ranking from the Japan Credit Ranking Agency, Ltd. (JCR). By this review, a full range of stakeholders such as students, their parents, faculty and members of the local community are assured of the reliability of university management (*Daigaku Keiei*) as defined in terms of fiscal reliability. This public stability provides the university with a competitive edge in the overall recruitment of students.

Cross-border education also benefits directly from quality assurance. Credit transfer for exchange students of the "Reconnaissance Japan Program" at J. F. Oberlin is a concrete example. This academic program for exchange students from overseas partner institutions is also extended to additional selected individual applicants who wish to learn more about Japan and experience it in person. Students may participate in Reconnaissance Japan for either a single semester or a full academic year. The program offers Japanese language skills and training courses along with a wide variety of culture and history courses on Japan taught in English and Chinese and offered each semester. Many students are in fact from China, and when they return to their home universities, J. F. Oberlin's substantial syllabi assure partner institutions of the quality of its courses and provide concrete grounds for the approval of credits earned by their students while in Japan. In addition, J. F. Oberlin recently implemented a new course numbering system for all subjects to provide additional transparency regarding the level and degree of difficulty of each course.

CONCLUSION: CHANGES IN UNIVERSITY MANAGEMENT CULTURE IN THE ERA OF MASS HIGHER EDUCATION

Beginning in 2004, MEXT has exerted strong national leadership in the area of quality assurance throughout Japan. From 2008 onwards, quality assurance as a process and set of outcomes has been embodied at the institutional level. This meets not only the demands of government policy but also those of universities themselves as they seek to meet both domestic and international standards that will assist approximating their goal of internal competitiveness. Quality assurance also allows universities to develop internal cultures of quality that can be tailored to their particular and individual missions. The original purpose of MEXT in promoting formal quality assurance is to prevent a drop in quality resulting from the relatively rapid quantitative expansion of the higher education system while also seeking to strengthen universities' educational capabilities.

However, compared to the period prior to 2004, activities related to quality assurance have effected various important changes in the management cultures of and for universities. First, the implementation of the third-party evaluation system has caused universities to pay much more attention to the standards mandated by MEXT in its aforementioned 2008 notice. In fact, the responsibility for institutions receiving a third-party evaluation periodically has changed the role of JUAA, NIAD-QE and JIHEE as they are regularly involved in universities' management. Second, the stakeholders who were previously members of the university management have now changed. Previously, universities managed their own affairs. Within the current system, university managers are required to pay much more attention to their students, students' parents and members of the local community in order to enhance their reliability among these critical reference groups. The results of evaluations conducted by JUAA, NIAD-QE and JIHEE, when positive, have become highly instrumental for increasing the credibility of reviewed universities. Finally, universities in Japan had been hidebound "ivory towers" forever 55 years, until the creation of the evaluation system in 2004. As discussed above, the historical combination of overcapacity among Japanese universities and a declining national birthrate fundamentally changed the nature of Japanese higher education. Universities were forced to improve the overall quality of the education they provided in order to survive, and the evaluation system provided the objective standards universities needed to achieve that goal.

In conclusion, quality assurance in Japanese higher education not only has ensured the public transparency and objectivity of universities but has also improved their ability to recruit students and gain needed recognition from overseas institutions. These quality assurance activities have also strengthened the overall educational capacities of the higher education system. One inescapable conclusion is that the effect of these external requirements has operated to change and improve the conventional culture of university management to the overall benefit of their institutions.

NOTES

1. JUAA is using several US accreditation agencies as a model. It started accrediting activities in 1951 for universities applying for full membership in JUAA, and revised its university accreditation system based on requesting a "self-study" by each university in 1996.

2. The same resolution was also approved at the 119th, 120th and 121st general meetings of APUJ in October 2003, March 2004 and October 2004, respectively. Available online at http://www.jihee.or.jp/en/about/objectives.html. Accessed: May 5, 2015.
3. For details, please refer to *2006 Year Edition MEXT White Paper*. Available online at http://www.mext.go.jp/b_menu/hakusho/html/hpab200601/002/003/006.htm. Accessed: May 8, 2015.
4. *The Japan Times.* "Japan and its birthrate: the beginning of the end or just a new beginning?" Available online at http://www.japantimes.co.jp/community/2016/02/10/voices/japan-birth-rate-beginning-end-just-new-beginning/#.V10cp9eyA7A. Accessed: May 6, 2016.
5. These are called Certified Evaluation and Accreditation Organizations in Japan.
6. The other is on school corporations for financial planning and management.
7. All full-time teaching staff is part of a research unit.
8. Twice a week, 180 minutes.

References

Central Council for Education. (2002). A report on building of a new system that affects the quality assurance of universities. Available online at http://www.mext.go.jp/b_menu/shingi/chukyo/chukyo0/toushin/020801.htm. Accessed 3 May 2015.

J. F. Oberlin Faculty Development Center. (2015). *J. F. Oberlin Faculty Development Center annual report.* Tokyo: J. F. Oberlin University.

MEXT. (2005). The future of higher education in Japan. Available online at: http://www.mext.go.jp/english/highered/1303556.htm. Accessed 25 April 2015.

MEXT. (2009). Quality assurance framework of higher education in Japan. Available online at: http://www.mext.go.jp/component/english/__icsFiles/afieldfile/2011/06/20/1307397_1.pdf. Accessed January 9, 2017.

MEXT. (2014). 2014 The basic school survey report (*Gakkō kihon chōsa: heisei 26 nendo (sōkuhō) kekka no gaiyō*). Available online at: http://www.mext.go.jp/b_menu/houdou/26/08/attach/1350731.htm. Accessed 1 April 2015.

Tachi, A. (2007). *Aratamete "Daigakuseido to wa nani ka" o tou.* Tokyo: Toshindo.

Umagoshi, T. (Ed.). (2004). *Higher education in Asia and Oceania.* Tokyo: Tamagawa Daigaku Shuppanbu.

CHAPTER 8

Quality Assurance and Quality Culture at a Public Higher Education Institution: A View from Within

Fauza Ab. Ghaffar and A. Abrizah

INTRODUCTION

Over the last few decades, the global higher education landscape has undergone rapid transformation. This transformation is characterized by the massification of higher education as reflected by the increased number of higher education institutions (HEIs) and higher education students, diversity in types and structure of HEIs and the growth of transborder educational institutions. Such development has led to the greater need for consistency and accountability of this sector. The changing scenario of higher education also leads to the need or demand for a change in the quality assurance (QA) mechanisms in the institutions, and thus, the push for a more systematic and formal quality movement at national and international levels.

In many countries or regions, the 1990s marked the beginning of the introduction of systematic quality management in the education sector

F.A. Ghaffar (✉) • A. Abrizah
Institute of Graduate Studies, University of Malaya,
Kuala Lumpur, Malaysia

© The Author(s) 2017
D.E. Neubauer, C. Gomes (eds.),
Quality Assurance in Asia-Pacific Universities,
DOI 10.1007/978-3-319-46109-0_8

121

(Vinzant and Vinzant 1996). Before this, the QA mechanisms between institutions and countries varied in nature, scope and purpose. In fact, the definition of the term "quality in education" was also elusive, ranging in its meaning and application from quality as being "excellent or exceptional, as being consistent, quality equated with customer satisfaction, as being value for money, as being fitness for purpose and also quality viewed as transformative" (Harvey and Knight 1996). However, since then, a consensus has gradually emerged that there is no "correct" definition, and thus, many of the definitions employed in practice may tend to be mutually exclusive.

In the context of the unprecedented growth and increased diversity of higher education providers in the Asia Pacific region, especially over the past decade and a half in the developing context of massification, for many countries QA has been regarded as primarily a suite of accountability mechanisms—thus the formulation of quality indicators largely reflecting minimum standards of performance, as well as the need for monitoring and reporting of institutions' performance in meeting those requirements. These quality indicators or requirements have focused primarily around the functions of the institutions, mainly teaching and learning, research and services supporting these core processes.

In many countries, the notion of accountability is related to the need "to account to some authority," often a central governmental entity for an institution's actions and activities. Jones (1992) noted the link of accountability to an authority and that the nature of the authority varies ranging from the central government to professional bodies or even independent quality-related agencies at the international, regional or national levels. In response to this proliferation of quality "authorities," one can observe the emergence of highly generalized quality frameworks or guidelines at the national and/or regional levels and the establishment of quality agencies in a wide variety of countries and across regions. These authorities often have come to act or play the role of external quality entities, and as the quality movement has matured, they have been complemented or even replaced in some countries by internal quality units or agencies established solely within an institution. These quality units or agencies, which act as the main drivers for quality within an institution, are usually subjected to monitoring by the external agencies.

Thus, currently one can observe not only the mushrooming of external quality agencies and regulatory bodies but also the proliferation of various approaches, mechanisms and QA systems instituted by a large number of higher education providers. The quality systems put in place vary considerably, and more importantly, perhaps the vigor and discipline that attach to QA activities differ across institutions and countries. The underlying argument of this chapter is that the QA activities of an institution tend to move progressively from the initial step of instituting a QA system, processes and procedures very much in response to the external requirements and aligned to external QA, to one in which internal QA activities play a more dominant role. At this stage, institutions may develop an internal quality culture adapted to their own institutional realities. These developments follow the presumption that the emergence of an institutional quality culture is meant to relate closely to the surrounding organizational culture and, more importantly, should be firmly based on shared beliefs, values expectations and commitments of those who constitute and populate an institution.

QA and the notion of a quality culture are interrelated. Some hold that a quality culture can be brought into being and be enforced by a system or structure put in place which would stimulate shared values and beliefs about the various dimensions of quality (Harvey and Stensaker 2008). However, they are not necessarily the same thing—an organization can have a quality assurance system (QAS) in place, but it does not necessarily result in the creation of a quality culture.

According to the European University Associations organization (EUA 2006), a quality culture is an organizational culture that aims to enhance quality permanently. Such a quality culture has two main characteristics: (a) a structural/managerial element with defined and formal QA processes and (b) an agent to coordinate individual quality efforts (QA) that gives rise to a cultural/psychological context of shared values, beliefs and commitment. By EUA's (2006) definition, the former is reflected through tools and processes to define, measure, evaluate and enhance quality; and the latter is reflected through personal commitment to strive for quality at the individual level, and through individual attitudes and awareness that add up to the culture at the collective level. As such, communication, participation and trust should be evident in an organizational quality culture. The idea of the model of a quality culture is that every quality development process has a comprehensive structural element and is carried out by actors who are committed, competent and understand quality as a relation which has to be realized in negotiation processes that will leave visible and invisible imprints in the organizational quality activities (Ehlers and Schneckenberg 2010).

Based on the premise that QA and a surrounding quality culture are two closely related processes and that QA is a component of quality culture (Loukkola and Zhang 2010), this chapter traces the evolution of the quality movement in Malaysia's first and oldest university—the University of Malaya (UM). More importantly, the authors will seek to make clear the relationship between QA and a quality culture and ascertain the level to which quality is embraced within the institution. In particular, we are concerned with the degree to which the routines and procedures employed to assess a system are merely that or whether practices have been developed and put in place with sufficient vitality for them to constitute the basis of what we may impute to be a quality culture. Within this sense of the process, QA has now become an important ingredient of the Malaysian Higher Education System.

The questions to be posed as the primary contribution of this chapter since QA's early implementation circa 2007 are: "How far has this system evolved?" and "Does it remain as merely quality assurance or has QA evolved into a culture?" These questions shall be analyzed in the context of the UM.

AN OVERVIEW OF QUALITY ASSURANCE IN MALAYSIAN HIGHER EDUCATION

Quality is an important issue in higher education in Malaysia. For the range of interested parties in the education process including all its stakeholders in one way or another, quality always has been important, although it was frequently taken for granted. Even on the eve of the contemporary "modern period," Hurley had pointed to a range of changed circumstances, including increased levels of participation, widening access, pressure on human and physical resources, the emergence of appraisal, audit and assessment mechanisms as having raised the profile of "quality" within the overall higher education endeavor (Hurley 1992). The quality of higher education has also been a long-standing concern for employers, in their roles as graduate recruiters and as research and training collaborators. Thus, since 1996, Malaysia has embarked on a formalized and structured system of QA in order to meet the challenges and concerns of these external constituencies. Prior to this, QA mechanisms were primarily institution-based, each institution putting in place or implementing its own rules, regulations or guidelines in an isolated and largely ad hoc manner. Overall, throughout the higher education environment, no monitoring system had been put in place to gauge the range and degree of whatever implementation of quality was taking place, thus making an effort to assess the effects of such mechanisms. For professional academic programs, QA was accomplished through program accreditation conducted by various professional bodies. The extent of "QA" activity that was taking place was in the degree to which public HEIs were subjected to regulations from Malaysia's Ministry of Education and the Public Service Department. In retrospect, given what was to come with the emergence of a more complete QA movement, such a regulatory regime was imperfect and incomplete.

The proliferation of private HEIs beginning in the late 1980s created doubts about the overall quality of higher education in the country, which led in turn to the establishment of the National Accreditation Board (LAN) in 1996. LAN, however, focused only on private institutions, and to provide for quality provision over the whole of Malaysian higher education in 2002, the Quality Assurance Division (QAD) of the Ministry of Education was established, which focused on public HEIs. However, different standards and practices concerning QA existed between the two agencies. Furthermore, it was evident that the QAD of the Ministry of Higher Education lacked the ability and capability especially in terms of resources and talent to carry out its function as an external quality agency.

With these developments, HEIs which had on their own initiative developed some form of QA were required to implement the Quality Management System (QMS) mainly based on the standards of the ISO: 9001. Most HEIs adopted some form of this system, albeit with varying scope for education (academic programs and teaching and learning), research or services. Till date, most institutions and universities have maintained their ISO certification.

In an effort to harmonize the QA of both private and the public HEIs, the Malaysian Qualifications Agency (MQA, http://www.mqa.gov.my/) was established in 2007 by merging the functions of the LAN and the QAD of the Ministry of Education. This event also marks the stipulation and enforcement of the Malaysian Qualifications Framework (MQF) with two complementary codes of practice: the Code of Practice for Programme Accreditation (COPPA) and the Code of Practice for Institutional Audit (COPIA). The role of the MQA was stipulated by the MQA Act 679 (Malaysia 2007) as:

The Agency shall be responsible for the implementation of the national frame-work to be known as the "Malaysian Qualifications Framework," consisting of qualifications, programmes and higher education providers based on a set of criteria and standards including learning outcomes achieved and credits based on students' academic load.

The establishment of both the MQA and the MQF marks an important milestone in the QA of Malaysian higher education. The framework provides a common benchmarking standard across all HEIs—thus creating important harmonization instruments at both programmatic and institutional levels. In implementing this function, MQA takes the approach of carrying out program accreditation and institutional assessments to ensure that programs offered meet and maintain the standards stipulated by COPPA. Meanwhile, concurrently, most institutions maintain the quality management system put in place earlier and are subject to both internal quality monitoring and external verification. Professional programs meanwhile are also subjected to the requirements of their respective professional bodies. Many programs also voluntarily subject themselves to national and external accreditation by various bodies.

Common to all QA systems and frameworks are the requirements of monitoring and improvement through an internal quality process instituted within the institution. This encourages institutions to establish their own internal quality agencies in the form of a department or unit or center charged with quality monitoring, especially in terms of assuring conformity to the external frameworks. In some ways, the size, resources and authority given to the institutional quality assurance (IQA) entity reflect the level of maturity of the institution's QA system and its commitment toward quality.

The work of the MQA revolves around two major approaches to assure quality in Malaysian higher education: the first approach is to accredit programs and qualifications; the second is to audit institutions or their components. Without compromising the quality of program accreditation practices, MQA started to empower the responsibilities of QA to HEIs by introducing a self-accrediting process. In 2010, the MQA carried out institutional audits. Based on the findings of these audits, eight institutions were given the status of being self-accreditated. These eight universities comprised four public HEIs and four branch campuses of foreign universities. By 2012, the number had increased to nine. The status of self-accreditation gives these universities the authority to accredit their own programs, and the MQA monitors them at regular intervals through institutional assessment. One of the major criteria and requirements for an institution to gain and retain this status is a stable and well-institutionalized IQA system and agency. This drive toward gaining self-accreditation has seen HEIs place considerable emphasis on enhancing their IQA system and agencies.

QUALITY ASSURANCE IN THE UNIVERSITY OF MALAYA

UM in Kuala Lumpur is the first and oldest institution of higher institution in Malaysia. UM is a comprehensive and intensive research-focused university. It is comprised of 12 faculties, 2 academies, 2 centers and 4 institutes—all these are regarded as academic centers of responsibility (CoR), and together they offer 111 undergraduate and 130 postgraduate programs. All these programs are MQF compliant and registered in the Malaysian Qualifications Registry (MQR)—a registry of MQA-accredited programs that ensures accredited higher education qualifications are registered and made available for reference to all stakeholders. UM employs about 2500 academic staff and serves a total of 22,500 students at an undergraduate: postgraduate ratio of about 1:1.06. As a research university, the desired ratio would be 1:2. About 5 and 10 percent of the undergraduate and postgraduate students, respectively, are international students. UM's international students come from 84 countries.

UM's quality system has evolved through several phases which may be categorized as conventional, transitional and transformational:

1. Conventional—period prior to the year 2000; characterized by institutional-based; isolated and ad hoc quality instruments and mechanisms of quality assurance;
2. Transitional—2000–2007; characterized by a formal, unified approach, holistic in nature based on national/international framework/standards/guidelines. During this period, UM implemented the QMS based on the MS ISO 9001:2000;
3. Transformational—2007 onward; enhancement of IQA and having gained the status of self-accreditation. Taking deliberate steps to bring about continual improvement in the effectiveness of the learning experience of students.

Since 2001, the implementation of the QMS has marked the beginning of a deliberate effort to fully gain the value of the QAS that was put in place. The UM-QMS is holistic and comprehensive in nature, which means that processes of certification cover all of its core processes which include teaching and learning, research and support services that encompass human resource utilization, infrastructure and assets, finance, commercialization, student affairs and library functions as well as sports and cultural services. Unlike many other universities, this certification is comprehensive; that is, the certification covers all the CoR of the university.

The implementation of QMS saw UM carrying out all the required activities of QA: documentation and records; customer satisfaction monitoring; internal quality control through internal audits, corrective, preventive actions and continual quality improvement. To date, UM has gone through six certifications and the QMS remains in place. It also forms the backbone for other QA requirements in teaching and learning, and research. The enforcement of the MQF in 2007 saw the expansion of the functions of the quality system to include reviewing the quality of academic programs and with the status of self-accreditation in 2010, in a manner and to a degree which would be conduced by an accreditation agency.

The existence of two main frameworks implemented in prior periods, that is, the ISO 9001:2000 and the MQF and its related standards, meant that UM was implementing yet another new approach to quality monitoring and assurance, that is, what the institution referred as an integrated approach based on a self-developed manual combining the requirements of the ISO and the MQF that allowed monitoring to be carried out simultaneously.

The above development has also been aligned with that of the internal QA agency in the university. This started as a quality committee reporting to a quality unit and is currently a quality center, a development that has resulted in changes in the nature of leadership and resources employed. At UM, the central agency is also supported by quality committees at the CoR, each headed by the deans or directors, who are in turn assisted by a quality manager, and a document controller, who are designated as quality champions and movers in their respective faculties/institutes/centers and academies.

To verify that the program is in compliance with MQF as well as to ascertain the appropriateness and adequacy of the program's educational arrangement as set by the code of practice, the university has undergone two institutional-based audits by panels appointed by the MQA. These are the self-accreditation audit of 2010 and a special postgraduate audit in

2013. On both occasions, the strength and authority of the IQA of UM were highlighted as indicated below by the self-accreditation audit:

- *"Given its strong and dynamic Quality Management System (QMS) with its 10 core processes on all aspects of teaching and learning in place UM has the QA system necessary for it to successfully pursue its vision & mission. There is also management commitment, staff acceptance at all levels, and the necessary internal control and monitoring systems for continual improvements throughout the system. The panel is assured of the University's commitment to Continual Quality Improvement (CQI)".*
- *"The MQA panel expresses appreciation of the University's efforts to embark on its Quality Journey in terms of internationally certified Quality Frameworks, about a decade ago".*
- *"The gradual but focused attention given to the internal quality assurance agenda is clear evidence that prominent organisational status is given continue quality improvement".*

(Excerpt from Academic Performance Audit Report by MQA Audit Panel 2010)

From the above testimony, it can be concluded that UM has put in place a strong and stable QAS with tools and processes to define, measure, evaluate, assure and enhance quality. The following are the traits of the University of Malaya Quality Assurance (UMQA):

1. Development of policies and procedures for each process based on both external and internal requirements.
2. A system of self-monitoring and evaluation. This is seen in terms of the internal audit process carried out at regular intervals based on a structured procedure and guidelines, supported by sufficient resources as in the employment of trained internal auditors. The annual and periodical thematic audit is commissioned from time to time by the top management and if often complemented by self-audits at the CoR.
3. Program self-assessment and self-accreditation based on the requirements of the MQF and related professional bodies.
4. Continual quality initiatives based on issues identified both from internal and external monitoring and assessment.
5. Still subjected to external monitoring from the respective related third-party agencies/bodies.

But the question at this juncture is: do all these procedures and initiatives add up to the university having created an internal quality culture?

Quality at the University of Malaya: Assurance or Culture?

Returning to the query posed at the beginning of this chapter, this is a question posed by virtually every Malaysian university as they seek to move beyond the formal requirements of externally directed quality reviews to the promotion of behaviors at every level of the organization that are framed and measured by their relative contribution of a commonly understood notion of quality. And while disciplined and concrete objective research has yet to be carried out to fully document this terrain, the following can be suggested as indicative of the direction that is emerging at UM:

1. External testimony from panels and fellow quality managers from other institutions indicate that UM has followed a remarkable journey in its quality endeavor and is considered as a showcase example of a quality system in place. This recognition is reflected in the various consultation requests with regard to the development of a QA system for a higher education institution from both internal and external universities.

2. The testimony and certification given by external bodies are another reflection of the university's success in its quality endeavor. Most external assessors are especially impressed by the university's success in maintaining the ISO certification, and professional accreditors often cite the quality of the program accredited to the systematic monitoring and documentation system put in place as a requirement of the QMS.

3. Self-monitoring has to a certain extent been a normal practice in the institution. Furthermore, corrective actions are also a norm, addressing the issues raised as a result of the various processes of self-monitoring. Quality within UM has been understood as to aim for continuous improvement, instead of ad hoc and instrumentalizing evaluations.

4. The management of the university is committed to and supports the quality initiatives—is reflected in the prominent authority, resources and support given to quality initiatives and requirements in all core processes of the university as well as the incentives and consideration given to quality involvement.

On the other hand, within this overall positive process some relevant issues remain. For example:

1. External versus Internal Drive

UM is still required and to a certain extent has chosen to rely on external standards and assessment. For example, there are voices suggesting that the university abandon its reliance on external audits and certification. The argument is made that if the QA system is stable and embraced by its subject population, it is sufficient that QA be managed, assured, monitored and improved based on internally driven motives, culture and initiatives. If this is the case, the argument is made, there is perhaps no need for further external certification.

As for the process of self-accreditation, UM still uses or depends on external standards. In actual fact, the argument is made, the university should be able to devise its own standards and code of practices—of course in line and perhaps above those of the MQF and its related documents/requirements. A question worth asking is: should UM go beyond the national requirements and take the initiative of defining its QA systems in a way that fits its own mission, objectives and values?

2. A bottom-up and top-down approach to quality

At UM, the top management and the quality managers are the major proponents of quality. Early on, it was a top-down process, and over the past 12 years, this seems to still be largely the case. Quality efforts taken are mostly reactive in nature usually responding to instructions from above or outside the university structure. One major concern is: has quality seeped through the various layers of the university's community, or does it remain the primary concern and business of management structures? Do the academics still see the QA processes as a burden with which they must comply? Do they experience ownership of the concept, or do they feel detached from it in their everyday activities?

3. Quality in Mind or on Paper?

In many ways this is the critical issue. Is there persuasive evidence that all aspects of quality are embraced by the university community? While one can point to some aspects such as those in administrative services where a quality framework appears to have been consolidated in the minds and spirits of the community, in other important areas such as in teaching and learning, it tends to remain a largely paper exercise. For example, in many aspects of the planning, implementing, assessing and evaluating within the teaching and learning processes, much improvement is needed to translate quality-informed processes to real effective decisions. There is a necessity to involve key stakeholders in program committees and to embrace a trend toward developing alumni relations and alumni questionnaires that would feed into quality discussions. The key question remains whether students have been consulted in a meaningful way such as in course planning and course development. So even within the relatively well-developed routines of the continually emergent quality culture at UM, the question remains whether the aspiration of quality has yet come to exist at the interpersonal level where its existence can be self-actuated beyond the reach of formal administrative means.

CONCLUSION

This chapter has sought to provide some insights from within the major Malaysian institution of higher education regarding the dynamic interplay between QA as a formal process and the daily operations of a quality culture. The internal insights are based on the authors' own experiences and observations with quality management at the institution level, as assessors/auditors for UM and other universities in the country, and also as actors in the formulation of quality policies and procedures at both the national and the university level.

Thus far, it is sufficient to conclude that Malaysian HEIs have traveled a long journey on the road to effective QA. UM is no exception. While it is safe to suggest that over the years the UM has put a commendable QA and management system in place, the journey toward building a more extensive quality culture continues. This is seen to be a challenging task in which part of the challenges are the exercise of academic freedom, the lack of shared vision and the prevailing culture of universities based on the privileging of individual autonomy which is often jealously guarded (Colling and Harvey 1995). As an old institution, UM definitely has faced and will continue to confront these challenges. However, the institution's mission is well set and clear, and the respective authorities are well aware of the challenges that face the newly crafted mission of the Quality Management and Enhancement Centre (QMEC, https://qmec2015.um.edu.my/) of UM, which coordinates all academic QA activities; monitors program audit documentation by the CoR; assists in the preparation of CoR institutional audit and program audits and makes quality everybody's business.

The development of a quality culture, and its implementation into organizational contexts viewed as a part of the overall organizational culture, has not yet developed a strong tradition in research and theory (Ehlers and Schneckenberg 2010). Ample evidence exists that QA demands the emergence of a broader view with respect to the development of the organization's quality culture. Such a development will entail the need for incorporating new values and negotiating future directions on the quality journey with the aim of rooting quality within rituals, symbols and the many diverse activities of the organization. To the present, little empirical work has been published in this very field. It is the intent of our further work to move on to the field of empirical research and seek to find and document evidence, good practices and methodologies that stimulate QA and root them in holistic approaches to the attainment of a quality culture.

REFERENCES

Colling, C., & Harvey, L. (1995). Quality control, assurance and assessment the link to continuous improvement. *Quality Assurance in Education, 3*(4), 30–34.

Ehlers, U.-D., & Schneckenberg, D. (2010). *Changing cultures in higher education*. Heidelberg/New York: Springer.

European University Association (EUA).(2006). *Quality culture in European universities: A bottom-up approach*. Brussels: European University Association.

Harvey, L., & Knight, P. (1996). *Transforming higher education*. London: Buckinham Society for Research into Higher Education and Open University Press.

Harvey, L., & Stensaker, B. (2008). Quality culture: Understandings,boundaries and linkages. *Europen Journal of Education, 43*(4), 427–442.

Hurley, B. (1992, April 6–8). *TQ implementation: Cultural issues and training*. Paper presented at the AETT Conference on 'Quality in Education', University of York.

Jones, G. W. (1992). The search for accountability. In S. Leach (Ed.), *Strengthening local government in the 1990s* (pp. 49–78). London: Longman.

Loukkola, T., & Zhang, T. (2010). *Examining quality culture Part 1: Quality assurance processes in higher education institutions* (European University Association—A research report). Brussels: European University Association.

Malaysia, Laws of. (2007). *Act 679 Malaysian Qualification Agency Act 2007*.

Vinzant, J. C., & Vinzant, D. H. (1996). Strategic management and total quality challenges and choices. *Public Administration Quarterly, 20*(2), 201–219.

PART II

Extending the Research of HE Quality Assurance

Creating a Culture of Quality: Navigating Change Toward a Culturally Responsive General Education Program

Valentina M. Abordonado

INTRODUCTION

The new general education program at Hawai'i Pacific University (HPU) is an example of organizational change that attempts to achieve greater permeability between the boundaries of the organization and the broader cultural context in which it is embedded. Specifically, it provides a liberal arts foundation set in the rich, cultural context of Hawai'i. It delivers diverse courses outside the major to inspire lifelong learning by introducing our students to ideas, perspectives, and experiences relevant to their lives. It envisions a unique curriculum to include the Hawaiian cultural context, HPU as the American gateway to Asia and the Pacific, an internationally diverse and engaged student body, and experiential learning rooted in a tropical island community.

To achieve this aim, HPU engaged its faculty in making quality improvements to the current general education program. In 2011, just shortly

V.M. Abordonado (✉)
General Education Program, Hawai'i Pacific University,
Honolulu, Hawaii, USA

© The Author(s) 2017
D.E. Neubauer, C. Gomes (eds.),
Quality Assurance in Asia-Pacific Universities,
DOI 10.1007/978-3-319-46109-0_9

before the conception of the new general education curriculum, our university welcomed a new university president, Dr. Geoffrey Bannister, who values shared governance between faculty and administration. He immediately focused on creating a student-centered university by cocreating a new university strategic plan with students, faculty, staff, and administration that was approved by the Board of Trustees in July 2012.

As part of the strategic planning process, HPU declared its mission as an international learning community set in the rich cultural context of Hawai'i where students from around the world join faculty and staff for an American education built on a liberal arts foundation, where our innovative graduate programs anticipate the changing needs of the community, and where we prepare our graduates to live, work, and learn as active members of a global society. HPU's vision was for a university that would be consistently ranked among the United States' top ten Western, independent, and comprehensive universities leveraging its geographic position between the Western and Eastern hemispheres and its relationship around the Pacific Rim to deliver an educational experience that is distinct among campuses (HPU General Education Program Revision Proposal, p. 13).

Our general education program sought to align itself with the university's mission and vision by declaring its intention to help students lead exultant and courageous lives as intelligent members of a complex society. The program does this by introducing students to different ways of knowing, challenging them to become creative and innovative both within their chosen career fields and in their wider lives, and by preparing them for the challenges and opportunities of the twenty-first century. The general education program further established its goal to provide its students with a liberal arts foundation set in the cultural context of Hawai'i by proposing courses that would inspire lifelong learning, introduce students to ideas, perspectives, and experiences relevant to their lives, and cultivate the skills, knowledge, and values expected of all educated persons (HPU General Education Program Revision Proposal, p. 13).

Responsiveness of the Initiative to Current Trends in Higher Education

In its efforts to achieve quality improvement, the general education program at HPU was designed to respond to current trends in higher education. The Lumina Foundation (2015) reports that, according to the most recent available data (2013), only 40 percent of working-age Americans (ages 25–64) have attained at least a two-year degree. Minority students fare even worse; degree attainment among Blacks is just 28 percent, among Native Americans just 23 percent, and among Hispanics just 20 percent. Further, the fiscal reality is that student loan debt has now surpassed 1 trillion dollars and the average tuition increases 8 percent a year (Chopra 2012; Kantrowitz 2012). Such debt presents a substantial burden to all graduates, especially those who choose to enter lower-paying public service careers, suffer setbacks such as unemployment or serious illness, or fail to complete their degree. The combination of poor student outcomes and increasing educational cost has led to additional scrutiny by the US Department of Education about institutional quality and a new emphasis on accountability for results from colleges and universities. In response to these trends, the Western Association of Schools and Colleges (WASC), which accredits Hawai'i Pacific University, revised its reaccreditation procedures in 2013, with an increased emphasis on standards and learning outcomes, student retention, and student graduation rates (WASC 2012).

In this way, WASC worked in concert with other regional accrediting bodies to ensure the achievement of the goals of a general education program, which the Association of American Colleges and Universities (2015) defines as a broad and multidisciplinary liberal education "deliberately designed to prepare all students for life, work, and citizenship by fostering their knowledge of the wider world (science, cultures, histories, societies, values) and by preparing them to think analytically and learn collaboratively" (v).

HPU's general education program had many models to select from within this broad charge; indeed, there are many approaches to providing students with a broad general education before they concentrate on their major. Many universities like Columbia, St. John's, and the University of Chicago, for instance, offer an extensive common core experience that cuts across disciplinary boundaries and centers on key economic, historical, literary, philosophical, and theological texts (Mintz 2014). Another approach to general education requires students to take courses across a spectrum of academic areas: the arts, the humanities, the social sciences, and the natural sciences. HPU incorporates this approach with courses in "The Creative Arts" (arts), "Traditions and Movements That Shape the World" (humanities), and "The Natural World" (natural sciences).

Yet another approach is to define the core curriculum thematically with topics such as cultural traditions, cultural change, social analyses, and moral reasoning. When these are combined with general introductory survey courses that emphasize breadth rather than specific content, students may develop the habits of mind and methodological approaches of diverse disciplines that enable them to think analytically and critically within particular disciplinary frameworks, such as Harvard's curriculum that seeks to "connect a student's liberal education—that is, an education conducted in a spirit of free inquiry, rewarding in its own right—to life beyond college" (Mintz 2014). HPU's new general education adopts this approach with thematic curriculum areas such as "Hawai'i and the Pacific," "The American Experience," "Global Crossroads and Diversity," "Technology and Innovation," and "The Sustainable World."

Finally, another approach emphasizes interdisciplinary learning experiences, commonly featuring a team-taught approach that involves faculty from diverse disciplines, such as the common core at Portland State University, which encourages students to make creative connections across disciplines, or the University of Texas Rio Grande, which provides a unified core focusing on a broad multidisciplinary theme (Mintz 2014). HPU's new general education curriculum envisions team-taught courses that take an experiential, multidisciplinary approach, but the courses within the identified curriculum areas have yet to achieve this vision.

Seemingly disconnected from these disciplinary or content-focused curricula are skills development courses common in most general education programs and favored by most regional accrediting agencies, such as those offered as part of HPU's new general education curriculum in "critical thinking," "written communication and information literacy," and "quantitative analysis and symbolic reasoning." Some universities try to integrate these skills development courses with content-focused courses with initiatives such as writing across the curriculum, or with alternative options, such as HPU's logic or statistics courses in lieu of more traditional quantitative reasoning courses. HPU also offers a first-year program that fosters learning communities, develops student leadership skills, acclimates first-year students to university life, and connects them to other students, faculty, and staff. Such personal contact with professors and cocurricular activities that foster high-impact, experiential learning strive to achieve greater student engagement and retention. HPU is also experimenting with online and hybrid learning models and have an election mechanism to provide a common core for all students, rather than a common core defined by particular colleges, such as the one at UC Berkeley.

What is remarkable about HPU is its expressed intent to educate the whole person and help students to achieve self-actualization by inspiring lifelong learning; by introducing our students to ideas, perspectives, and experiences relevant to their lives; by challenging them to become creative and innovative both within their chosen career fields and their wider lives; and by preparing them for the challenges and opportunities of the twenty-first century.

More work remains to be done in this area as the education of the whole person also attempts "to cultivate students' social, emotional, physical, and ethical development and to foster creativity, promote psychological well-being, stimulate a rich and thoughtful interior life, explore core beliefs, encourage social engagement, and cultivate empathy and an ethic of service and caring" (Mintz 2014). HPU's general education program envisions increased opportunities for service learning and civic engagement, and cocurricular activities that encourage dialogue about social, cultural, political, and global concerns. These opportunities, along with other high-impact practices, such as first-year seminars, learning communities, writing intensive courses, collaborative assignments and projects, undergraduate research, diversity/global learning seminars, internships, and capstone courses and projects, will help us achieve a holistic general education program that is not only multidisciplinary but also multidimensional.

RELATIONSHIP OF THE INITIATIVE TO THE QUALITY MOVEMENT

This initiative has reflected the philosophy of the quality continuous improvement model, which is a data-driven, systematic, and process-focused approach to planning, doing, studying, and acting. Specifically, it subscribed to the seven-step Shewhart cycle (Ishikawa circle): identifying an improvement opportunity, evaluating the problem and setting a target for improvement, analyzing the root causes of the problem, planning and implementing actions to correct the root causes, studying the results to confirm that the actions achieve the target, maintaining the improved level of performance, and planning for the future.

At its disposal were a host of analytical tools for generating ideas, making decisions, analyzing problems, and analyzing data (AFQI 1993).

HPU's interest in the quality improvement process was inspired by its enduring interest in the scholarship of teaching and learning. Interestingly, one of the preferred methods of inquiry for the scholarship of teaching and learning is action research, which parallels many of the quality improvement steps described above. Indeed, this process of defining the variables and research questions; collecting, analyzing, and interpreting data; and finally, planning the next action steps closely aligns with the quality continuous improvement process (Mills 2014). Such research is less concerned with matters of external validity or the degree to which the study results are generalizable or applicable to groups and environments outside of the research setting. Rather, action research scholars, such as Kincheloe (1991), ask: "Is 'trustworthiness' a more appropriate word to use?" (p. 135). Similarly, Wolcott (1994) suggests, "...'understanding' seems to encapsulate the idea as well as any other everyday term" (p. 367). In the same way, Greenwood and Levin (2000) argue that, because action researchers do not make claims to context-free knowledge (i.e. action research by its very nature is based in the context for learning), issues of credibility, validity, and reliability are measured by the willingness of researchers and stakeholders "to act on the results of the action research" (p. 98). In short, like continuous quality improvement, the validity of action research "depends on whether the solution to the problem (the planned intervention or improvement) actually solves the problem" (Mills, p. 115).

HPU's new general education program has made significant strides toward continuous quality improvements. It has reduced the complexity of its structure, program, and the number of learning outcomes from 44 learning outcomes to just 13, making the assessment process less onerous and time-consuming. Importantly, it has also reduced the number of credits required for graduation from 124 to 120, and the general education credit requirements from 57 to 36, making it possible for students to graduate in four years while pursuing a double major or a minor and engaging in high-impact experiences, such as research, internships, and study abroad. These reductions have also increased the number of available unrestricted electives and dramatically decreased time to graduation for transfer students and students needing to take developmental courses. In this way, HPU has eliminated one of the biggest barriers to graduation observed by Christensen and Eyring (2011), which is a problematic mixture of excessive credits required for graduation, the major, and general education that create graduation delays for students. Jones and Wellman (2009) suggest that this more prescribed path through a narrower and more coherent range of curriculum options leads to better retention, since advising is more straightforward, scheduling is easier to predict, and students are less likely to get lost in the process. For, as Gaston and Gaff (2009) remind us, "When students routinely discuss the general education program as a set of requirements that must be endured before meaningful study can begin, it should be clear that the opportunity of a generation has been missed."

To a certain extent, the new general education curriculum strives to reduce the competition among programs for enrollment numbers. Such a mind-set leads to a more faculty- and program-centered approach than to a student-centered approach. While a certain amount of competition for courses still exists, limiting the number of courses in each curriculum area to six to eight substantially reduces this rivalry among programs. Further, the decision not to make significant structural changes to the new general education program for the first two years allows HPU to make data-driven, evidence-based decisions about the optimal number and type of course to offer in each curriculum area.

Importantly, changes to this point have utilized the familiar tools of quality improvement. These have included faculty surveys; student surveys; student focus groups; multiple program meetings; university strategic planning meetings and study groups; data collection and research; meetings with executive, administrative, faculty, staff, and student stakeholders; campus visits to other universities and institutions; attendance and presentations at WASC and Association of American College and Universities (AACU) meetings, workshops, and conferences; informal "talk story" meetings with multiple stakeholders; analyses of other general education programs, creation of a wiki Web site, hosting of a conference for faculty and staff; and working and advisory group meetings. These activities preceded multiple drafts and positive feedback from faculty, student, and administration on a strategic implementation plan that proposed a new mission statement, a new purpose statement, three program objectives, 11 curriculum areas, 13 student learning outcomes, and 12 courses, and a budgetary plan to support resource requirements. In addition to special faculty forums, a faculty retreat, and multilevel curricular approval meetings, this process also established and expanded multiple community partnerships to support the civic engagement learning outcome requirement for two curriculum areas (Hawai'i and the Pacific and The Sustainable World). Many of these interesting partnerships, fostered through the Native Hawaiian Speakers'series, have been lost with the departure of the former Assistant Dean for General Education and chief architect of this program, but a Hawai'i and Pacific Speakers' series planned for fall 2015 will restore some of this emphasis, which will be critical to delivering a culturally responsive program.

In sum, the critical challenges emerging from the analysis of this quality improvement to the current general education program include the need for faculty across disciplines, departments, and colleges to collaborate, to develop and to deliver robust and authentic assessments of student learning as measured by criteria-based analytic rubrics that will lend themselves to analysis of findings and continuous, curricular improvement. To this end, in fall 2015, the HPU's general education program launched an institution-wide assessment system, supported by a powerful software tool.

In addition, the new general education initiative needs to achieve a truly multidimensional stature that provides more multidisciplinary, team-taught, and experiential courses, increased opportunities for service learning and civic engagement, and cocurricular activities that encourage dialogue about social, cultural, political, and global concerns. To this end, the HPU general education program continued the cocurricular viewpoints film series and launched a Hawai'i and Pacific Speakers' series.

General Education as a Culturally Responsive Curriculum

As a culturally responsive curriculum, HPU's general education program is distinct from some of the earliest iterations of the quality movement, which is devoid of any reference to cultural contexts. Indeed, this flaw in the quality improvement model is curious, particularly since it has been argued that culture is, in fact, the salient feature in any human interaction (Abordonado 1998). To be completely fair, the quality movement at that time did speak about organizational culture as "a common set of values, beliefs, attitudes perceptions and accepted behaviors shared by individuals within an organization" (AFQI 1993, p. 97). Similarly, it also referred to culture change as "a major shift in attitudes, norms, sentiments, beliefs, values, operating principles and behavior of an organization" (AFQI 1993, p. 97). Nevertheless, it paid little attention to how the organizational culture mirrors the broader cultural context in which it is embedded.

HPU's new general education program will distinguish itself by attending to the rich, cultural context in which it is embedded by promoting culturally responsive teaching strategies, especially in curriculum areas such as Hawai'i and the Pacific and the Sustainable World. Gay (2000) defines culturally responsive teaching as using the cultural knowledge, prior experiences, and performance styles of diverse students to make learning more appropriate and effective for them by teaching to and through the strengths of these students. According to Gay (2010), culturally responsive teaching is validating, comprehensive, multidimensional, empowering, transformative, and emancipatory. Such an approach is especially relevant for HPU, which has been ranked No. 1 in overall diversity nationwide, based on ethnic, geographic, and gender diversity of the student body, thereby validating HPU's reputation as a global gathering place.

Key characteristics of culturally responsive teaching for general education would include:

- Acknowledging the legitimacy of the cultural heritages of different ethnic groups, both as legacies that affect students' dispositions, attitudes, and approaches to learning and as worthy content to be taught in the formal curriculum.
- Building bridges of meaningfulness between home and school experiences as well as between academic abstractions and lived sociocultural realities.
- Using of a wide variety of instructional strategies that are connected to different learning styles.
- Encouraging students to know and praise their own and each other's cultural heritages.
- Incorporating multicultural information, resources, and materials in all the subjects and skills routinely taught in schools. (Gay 2010)

Such a curriculum would attempt to teach *through* native knowledge in the content areas, rather than teaching about it. Specifically, it would engage students in values-driven, place-based, and object-oriented projects in the classroom, using proven instructional strategies and assessment techniques that work well with diverse students.

The intent of such a culturally responsive, experiential curriculum would be to provide a positive climate for inquiry and problem posing and to engage students in self-directed investigations. This experiential curriculum would provide for personally meaningful and self-initiated involvement and evaluation that would facilitate a pervasive change in the students' understanding of and attitudes toward the Hawaiian and Pacific languages, cultures, and history. To create a positive climate for learning, it would make available learning resources, balance both the intellectual and affective components of learning, and engage students in learning in a risk-free environment.

This experiential curriculum would be fully integrated into the academic curricula, highlight reflection, and foster an ethic of social and civic responsibility and would add depth to the students' educational experience and provide interdisciplinary opportunities for collaboration. This experience would promote learning among students and strengthen their bonds as an international community of learners.

Values-Driven *A'o* is the word for education in the Hawaiian language, but it means much more. It implies both to learn (*a'o mai*) and to teach (*a'o aku*). These concepts embody the notion that, as one learns and becomes skilled (mastery), knowledge and skill are to be used and shared with others (generosity). To this end, students would first learn about the Hawaiian and Pacific cultures, history, and languages through a series of experiential learning experiences provided by learned scholars from the cultural community. Then, students would share the knowledge, skills, and values that they have learned through this curriculum. Specifically, they would collaborate to create integrated projects designed to preserve, protect, and perpetuate Hawaiian and Pacific cultures, languages, and history.

Five Hawaiian values would form the philosophical and knowledge base, which would guide students' interactions with each other as they engage in place-based learning activities:

- *'Imi Na'auao*—to seek knowledge. The value of *'Imi Na'auao* promotes the ideal of lifelong learning.
- *Ho'ihi*—to respect. *Ho'ihi* is the value of respect; it teaches us to honor the dignity of others and to conduct ourselves with integrity.
- *Laulima*—to work cooperatively. The value of *laulima* encourages collaboration and cooperation.
- *Malama*—to care for. *Malama* is the benevolent value of stewardship.
- *Pono*—to be moral and proper. *Pono* is the personal and professional value of rightness and balance.

Place-Based Hawaiian and Pacific place-based learning looks at the *'āina* (land) and local environment from a native perspective to study how it has been used over time, modern land use issues, and the relationships among place, history, culture, and tradition. Throughout such a curriculum, students would engage in place-based learning strategies, using Hawaiian and Pacific settings to make connections to their cultures, languages, and history. Learning activities would include field trips, classroom displays, guest speakers, and lessons that investigate their linguistic, cultural, and historical traditions.

Object-Oriented From maps and photographs to documents and artifacts, primary sources provide vital clues to the language, culture, and history of Hawai'i and the Pacific. Throughout this curriculum, students would examine primary sources to learn what they reveal about the historical, cultural, and linguistic traditions of Hawai'i. As they investigate and analyze primary sources, they would also explore the learning strategies designed to bring the Hawaiian and Pacific languages, cultures, and history to life.

Hawaiian and Pacific Teaching and Learning Strategies Throughout this experiential curriculum, students would engage in five processes that constitute traditional patterns of teaching and learning in the Hawaiian and Pacific cultures. Based on the work of Mary Kawena Pukui (1983), the Hawaii Alive Project (2011) led by the Bishop Museum articulated these processes as Hawaiian teaching strategies:

- *Nānā ka maka* (The eye sees). The learner observes the task to be done, while the teacher models or demonstrates the task.
- *Hoʻolohe ka pepeiao* (The ear listens). The learner listens to the teacher's instructions and any other sounds that clarify the task (wind, rain, ocean, or materials being used). Not all of the teacher's instructions are with words.
- *Paʻa ka waha* (Secure/shut/fasten the mouth). During this critical thinking stage, the learner is silent and processes the two previous steps.
- *Hana ka lima* (Put the hands to work). The learner learns by doing by mimicking the teacher's work. The teacher observes and checks the student's work.
- *Nīnau* (Question). The learner asks questions only after achieving or approaching proficiency in the previous steps. The teacher may send the learner back to the previous steps again to self-correct.

By grounding these teaching strategies in the values, norms, beliefs, and practices of the culture, educators can improve the educational experiences, achievement, and socio-emotional well-being of their students.

In sum, a vision for a culturally responsive general education curriculum would be one that would enable our students to achieve an understanding of their own sociocultural settings, respect and learn from those who do not share our values and cultural orientations, and interact with members of a global community. The goal for our students would be what Glover and Friedman (2015) refers to as transcultural competence, which allows the educated, global citizen to adapt to diverse sociocultural settings, often without prior knowledge of the specific cultures involved. Our students would not only recognize and respect cultural differences but also reconcile and realize these cultural differences as opportunities for problem solving, innovation, and change.

References

Abordonado, V. M. (1998). *The effect of gender on linguistic politeness in written discourse*. Dissertation, Tucson, Arizona, University of Arizona.

Air Force Quality Institute. (1993). *Process improvement guide: Quality tools for today's Air Force* (2 ed.). Alabama: Maxwell Air Force Base/Air University.

Association of American Colleges and Universities. (2015). *General education maps and markers: Designing meaningful pathways to student achievement*. Washington, DC: Association of American Colleges and Universities.

Bishop Museum. (2011). Hawaiian teaching strategies. *Hawai'i Alive*. Retrieved from http://hawaiialive.org.

Chopra, R. (2012). Too big to fail: Student debt hits a trillion. Retrieved from the Consumer Financial Protection Bureau website: http://www.consumerfinance.gov/blog/too-big-to-fail-student-debt-hits-a-trillion/

Christensen, C. M., & Eyring, H. J. (2011). *The innovative university: Changing the DNA of higher education from the inside out*. San Francisco: Jossey-Bass.

Gaston, P. L., & Gaff, J. G. (2009). *Revising general education and avoiding the potholes*. Washington, DC: Association of American Colleges and Universities.

Gay, G. (2000). *Culturally responsive teaching: Theory, research and practice*. New York: Teachers College Press.

Gay, G. (2010). *Culturally responsive teaching: Theory, research, and practice* (2 ed.). New York: Teachers College Press.

General Education Program Revision Proposal. (2013, August 28). Honolulu: Hawai'i Pacific University.

Glover, J., & Friedman, H. (2015). *Transcultural competence: Navigating cultural differences in the global community*. Washington, DC: American Psychological Association.

Greenwood, D. J., & Levin, M. (2000). Reconstructing the relationships between universities and societies in through action research. In N. K. Denzin & Y. S. Lincoln (Eds.), *Handbook of qualitative research* (2 ed., pp. 85–106). Thousand Oaks: Sage.

Jones, D., & Wellman, J. (2009). Rethinking conventional wisdom about higher education finance. Retrieved from the National Center for Higher Education Management Systems and Delta Cost Project website: http://www.deltacostproject.org/resources/pdf/advisory_10_Myths.pdf

Kantrowitz, M. (2012). Tuition inflation. Retrieved from the FinAid website: http://www.finaid.org/savings/tuition-inflation.phtml

Kincheloe, J. (1991). *Teachers as researchers: Qualitative inquiry as a path to empowerment*. Philadelphia: Falmer.

Lumina Foundation for Education. (2015). A stronger nation through higher education. Retrieved from the Lumina Foundation for Education website: http://strongernation.luminafoundation.org/report.

Mills, G. E. (2014). *Action research: A guide for the teacher researcher* (5 ed.). New York: Pearson.

Mintz, S. (2014, October 27). Educating the whole person. *Inside Higher Education*. http://www.insidehigereducation.com

Pukui, M. K. (1983). '*Ōlelo Noʻeau, proverbs and poetical sayings, Bernice P. Bishop Museum special publication no. 71*. Honolulu: Bishop Museum Press.

Western Association of Schools and Colleges (WASC). (2012). 2013 handbook of accreditation. Retrieved from WASC website: http://wascsenior.org/content/draft-2013-handbook-accreditation

Wolcott, H. F. (1994). *Transforming qualitative data: Description, analysis, and interpretation*. Thousand Oaks: Sage.

CHAPTER 10

Casting the Net Wider: Coping with an Increasingly Diverse International Student Body in Australia

Catherine Gomes

INTRODUCTION

As an export industry, international education in Australia is a powerhouse, bringing in $19 billion in full fees and associated expenditures in 2015 alone while impacting on secondary industries such as rental accommodation, hospitality and tourism. The international education sector, moreover, currently employs more than 130,000 people. Recognizing the significance of international education, on 30 April 2016, Richard Colbeck, the then-Minister for International Education and Training, released a long-term roadmap known as the *National Strategy for International Education 2025* to drive the sector for the ensuring decade. The strategy was first circulated as a draft a year earlier in April 2015 in order to gain feedback from international education stakeholders (Australian Government 2015). The aim of the strategy, as Minister Colbeck notes, is to strengthen and solidify international education as "one of the five super growth sectors

C. Gomes (✉)
School of Media and Communication, RMIT University,
Melbourne, Australia

© The Author(s) 2017
D.E. Neubauer, C. Gomes (eds.),
Quality Assurance in Asia-Pacific Universities,
DOI 10.1007/978-3-319-46109-0_10

contributing to Australia's transition from a resources-based to a modern services economy" and to "ensure Australia remains a leader in the provision of education services to overseas students" (Australian Government, v). In addition, the strategy points to the ongoing benefits from this sector in terms of the bridges it builds between Australia and the rest of the world and particularly highlights the collaborative ventures Australia has overseas because of international education through research, trade, investment and social engagement. One of the most significant recommendations was to increase international student numbers from the current half a million to 990,000 by 2025.

While the strategy generally acknowledges the significance of international education and international students to the economy and to the future of Australia's engagement with Asia—the region where the majority of current international students come from—it does not acknowledge or discuss the impact that increasing numbers of students have on institutions and on the wider community. Reflecting on these issues, I provide some practical applications, which I have used in my large and diverse courses to show that the diversity of increasing numbers of international (and local) students provides an excellent opportunity for blending both international and local perspectives into the curriculum. I also point out though that while there are positive outcomes to gain within the curriculum, the real challenge of the increasing international student intake takes place outside the classroom. The rising presence of international students has caused undue tensions in Australia, with the media and the public typecasting them within unfair frameworks. Here I address these public and media concerns directly with evidence from my own ongoing research into the international student experience in Australia.

NATIONAL STRATEGY

So what are the key elements of the Australian government's national strategy on international education? Recognizing the potential to take the international education industry to the next level in order to make it one of the mainstays of the Australian economy, in what then-International Education Minister Colbert explains as "one of the five super growth sectors contributing to Australia's transition from a resources-based to a modern services economy" (Australian Government 2016, p. v), the strategy recommends expanding international education beyond the Asian region.

It advocates that the sector needs to look for emerging markets while still recruiting from the traditional sources of China, India and Southeast Asia. The reason why the strategy suggests recruiting from outside Asia is a fear that the markets there have become saturated. Potential international students from Asia now have the option of not leaving the region but enrolling in other Asian nations for their qualifications. Emerging yet dynamic regional hubs of China, Taiwan, South Korea, Japan, Indonesia, Singapore and Malaysia are becoming attractive destinations for Asian and non-Asian students (e.g. from the Middle East; UNESCO 2016). These new education hubs are a direct threat to Australia's billion-dollar education industry and its secondary industries. In 2013, these regional hubs combined, hosted 7 per cent of the global share of international students, edging out Australia, which only had 6 per cent of the market share (UNESCO 2016). Malaysia, for instance, has plans to increase its international student intake to 200,000 by 2020 (Hughes 2015). Countries such as Malaysia and Singapore are also attractive because of the prospect of the availability of local jobs after graduation. Potential new markets such as those in Latin America and the Middle East, which were highlighted in a previous draft of the national strategy (Australian Government 2015, pp. 8 & 26), are attractive targets because of the growing middle class in these regions. A strong middle class, as the previous draft of the strategy explained, would mean a growing number of families able to afford an overseas education for their children (Australian Government 2015, pp. 8 & 26). Recruiting from emerging markets is also a fail-safe position to attract increasing numbers of young people to Australia looking to improve their educational qualifications. The recruiting of new students stems too from a fear of an oversaturation of the established markets in Asia since the strategy also reads international education as a two-way process in which Australia not only exports international education, but also sends its own students overseas in order to build bridges with host nations through schemes such as the New Colombo Plan (Department of Foreign Affairs and Trade 2016).

In order to accomplish all this and thereby strengthening Australia's position as an international education giant in this competitive yet lucrative industry, the strategy provides a multipronged approach around three pillars. The first pillar known as "strengthening the fundamentals" will be achieved by building on Australia's current education, training and research system, providing students with the best education experience possible and keeping check on quality assurance and regulation. The second pillar "making transformative partnerships" aims to strengthen (educational and research) partnerships both at home and abroad as well as with alumni, in addition to enhancing local and international student, educator and researcher mobility. The final pillar sees Australia "competing globally" by promoting the country as a high-quality international education destination and by creating opportunities for further growth of the international education sector (e.g. in regional Australia; Australian Government 2016, p. 11).

In order to achieve these goals, the strategy, among other things, commits the federal government to work with state and territory governments, stakeholders, businesses and the wider community. So what are the positives that we can take out of the strategy?

Value Placed on Industry and International Students

Asian-born international students after all have had a presence in Australia ever since the commencement of the Colombo Plan in 1951 when soon-to-be decolonized nations and former colonies in the British Commonwealth sent sponsored students to be trained in skills that would assist in the economic, infrastructural and social development of these nations. By the 1980s, Australia had become a global player in the export of education by offering courses and qualifications that attracted students from Southeast Asia and, increasingly, from Northeast Asia and South Asia. In 2016, education services brought in close to AUD$21 billion through full-fee-paying international students.[1] By the end of 2015, 525,172 international students (including exchange students) were enrolled in educational institutions throughout Australia (Australian Department of Education and Training 2015). Most of these students came from a range of different countries from Asia, the Middle East and elsewhere. However, the majority of international students came from Asia, with the top countries being China (136,097), India (53,568), Vietnam (21,807), the Republic of Korea (20,790) and Malaysia (20,641) (Australian Department of Education and Training 2016). While high school-going international students in Australia were also plentiful, their numbers have not been comparable to those who are undertaking postsecondary study in universities, vocational education and training (VET) institutes and English Language Intensive Courses for Overseas Students (ELICOS) colleges. International students today inhabit Australian cities and towns (e.g. Armidale in New South Wales), supporting higher education institutions and high schools.

International students in higher education further contribute to the Australian economy through casual and seasonal employment. As a condition of their visas, international students are not allowed to hold full-time permanent jobs, since that would require a separate working visa. International students, however, are allowed to work a total of 40 hours per fortnight (Department of Immigration and Border Protection 2014). This means that they usually work part-time in contract or non-contract positions. International students often work in retail, hospitality, tourism, agriculture (e.g. fruit-picking), sales and telemarketing, administration or tutoring. Postgraduate international students, particularly doctoral candidates, often take on sessional tutoring jobs at universities (Australian Trade Commission 2016). In 2009–2010, the median weekly income of students in employment was AUD$564 (Australian Bureau of Statistics 2013). International students work primarily to support themselves since international student fees are high. At the time of writing, an undergraduate degree costs between AUD$15,000 and AUD$33,000, a postgraduate degree between AUD$20,000 and AUD$37,000, and a doctoral degree between AUD$14,000 and AUD$37,000 (Australian Trade Commission 2016). Meanwhile, the estimated cost of living in a shared student apartment in the city of Melbourne was AUD$23,000 to AUD$31,000 per annum in 2016 (Student Services, The University of Melbourne 2016).

In the meantime, approximately one in five (22 per cent) of all tertiary students were international students, with the states of New South Wales and Victoria supporting the largest number of students, with a combined share of 58 per cent of the entire Australian market (Australian Bureau of Statistics 2011). Fifty-five per cent of the combined New South Wales and Victorian international student population live and study in Melbourne alone (City of Melbourne 2013). These international students attend the universities, VET institutes and ELICOS colleges within the city and occupy residential apartments in the heart of the central business district. The strategy is not wrong in its assumptions of the positive impact international students have on the Australian economy.

While the strategy is no doubt aspirational and driven by economic interests, it was heartening to read its acknowledgement of the value of the sector and the benefits international students bring to Australia. The strategy, for instance, is committed to building bridges between Australia and the rest of the world through international education as noted in the following statement:

It offers opportunities to build enhanced bilateral and multilateral relationships, which increase cultural awareness and social engagement. In addition, diplomacy is advanced through Australian educated alumni who develop lasting connections at personal, organisational and government levels. All of this is fostering better relationships with our regional neighbours and the rest of the world. (Australian Government 2016, p. 7)

Doing so allows the broader population to understand international students and their contributions to Australia better. Perhaps the most obvious question to raise is, what impact does the strategy potentially have on institutions?

The Challenge of Increasing Numbers and Diversity, and What Can Be Done

The strategy maps out the benefits of expanding the international education sector by providing strategies for attracting international students to Australia. However, what the strategy does not do is suggest the ways in which institutions will be supported to meet increasing numbers of diverse students on their campuses. What can institutions do in this case, and what are the overall implications for quality issues in general and the pursuit of quality cultures particularly at the campus level?

Providing All Students with Both Global and Local Perspectives

One of the challenges institutions face is supporting staff to negotiate through large and increasingly multicultural classrooms in both the real as well as virtual spaces. Work in the area of international student engagement in the classroom is readily available as resources and educators need to be pointed toward these areas. Organizations such as ISANA: International Education Association, which represent professionals in Australia and New Zealand working in international student services, advocacy and teaching and policy development in international education, conduct yearly conferences with cutting-edge research into international education and international student issues. In 2010, a group of Melbourne-based academics from the University of Melbourne and RMIT University provided a groundbreaking report on how to engage with international students in the classroom. Led by Sophie Arkoudis, the report, called *Finding common ground: Enhancing interaction between domestic and international students*, provides an effective and practical guide to harnessing diversity in the classroom by promoting "interaction between students from diverse cultural and linguistic backgrounds" (Arkoudis et al. 2010, p. 6).

In general, universities also need to encourage and support staff in creating courses that allow for this range of international diversity to shine through. By diversity, domestic students should also be included into this conversation. Here using real-world examples from the regions and students' host countries would enhance the learning experience (McLoughlin and Lee 2009). While Australian institutions and students unquestionably provide international students with local perspectives, international students are able to repay in kind given sufficient opportunities. Much is gained within academic settings if international students can be seen as far more than merely consumers of an educational "product" but rather as drivers of a global outlook within the content of current and future courses. International students can provide local students with global perspectives both incidentally (e.g. through classroom discussions) as well as directly (e.g. through course material). With this merger of student populations and pedagogic intentions, both local and international students can be prepared for future employability in the global workforce. Moreover, the incorporation of both local and international examples is something I use in my own teaching to encourage more student interaction plus increasing both local and international students' knowledge of each other's cultural and social environments.

A Case Study of Teaching Large and Diverse Classes in the Humanities

Since joining the School of Media and Communication at RMIT in 2007, I have been fortunate enough to teach at various times in the School of Media and Communication exciting humanities courses to large and diverse student cohorts in different programmes such as the Asian Media and Culture (AMC) Major, the Communication Strand, the Singapore Mass Communication programme and the Master of Communication programme. I have, in other words, been developing, coordinating and teaching courses at the undergraduate (first to third year) and postgraduate levels, in onshore and offshore programmes, and to students from all the professional programmes in the Bachelor of Communication. In each programme, I further encounter large and diverse student bodies with my courses enrolling between 80 and 500 students. The mode of delivery of my courses is lecture-tutorial style. While the lecture includes all enrolled students, each tutorial is made up of no fewer than 25 students. Approximately half of my students are international students from Asia who predominantly come from Southeast Asia (Singapore, Malaysia, Indonesia and Vietnam) and Mainland China.

Maintaining quality assurance standards for such large, culturally and nationally diverse cohorts is challenging but not impossible. Here, I develop courses which arm students with theoretical frameworks and real-world examples in order to push them to critically engage with cultural artefacts while providing timely and generous feedback on assessments. The development of courses goes hand in hand with maintaining good communication with tutoring staff. The professional relationship between course coordinator and tutoring staff is vital in teaching large and diverse cohorts. To develop and maintain this relationship, I am in ongoing email contact with tutoring staff. I also have regular weekly meetings to discuss any issues with the course material or with students that develop in class. These weekly meetings are beneficial in providing support for tutoring staff since the majority of them are casual staff themselves engaging in postgraduate study (e.g. master's and doctoral research students). While I do not micromanage my tutors when it comes to the ways in which they run their tutorials, I provide them with weekly tutorial outlines (e.g. leading questions and learning activities for mass student participation) that assist them to maintain quality standards. Allowing tutors some independence in how they run their tutorials is crucial for their own development as teachers and as future university lecturers.

As the objectives of the courses I teach are to make students aware of Asia in the AMC Major and to critically investigate Australian, particularly indigenous, cultural artefacts in the Communication Strand courses, I make frequent use of material from everyday culture and life such as visual images and soundtracks sourced from different media that include film, television and the Internet. I also take students on field trips and introduce them to significant members of the community in order to critically engage and contextualize the themes of the course. To make sure that the objectives of these courses are met, assessments are designed to test students on their ability to read and critically engage with both the set readings and the wider scholarship and to use the concepts that they learn and apply them to the cultural texts which they choose. Here key concepts are emphasized and students have the freedom to choose cultural artefacts and apply these concepts in their analysis. Since weekly tutorials are two hours long, part of the time is converted into workshops to help students with their work-in-progress assignments. Students sit in groups and discuss their work-in-progress assignments with their tutor and with their group. Generous feedback and support thus are provided by both tutor and peers. Students in other words are academically supported throughout the course.

Asia comes alive in the AMC Major with courses such as Modern Asia, Sex and Gender in Asia, and Adventures in Asian Popular Culture. Here I not only refer to media artefacts (adding to the traditional list new arrivals on the scene like social media and mobile phone technology) but also on student experiences of Asia. My AMC Major courses, which often see 80 to 170 students enrolled, emphasize that Asia is around us and not solely a geographical "alien" mass but rather one that is very much part of every student's daily life. The Asian international students enjoy the familiarity of Asia while discovering new things about their region through lecture and tutorial discussions. Local students realize that Asia is not north of Australia but around them in terms of their consumption of Asia through media, fashion and food. The week we look at food in Modern Asia, I bring different kinds of Asian snacks to class while the lecture uses the case study of Thai restaurants, which promise a taste of Thailand overseas. Students realize that global forces of transnationalism have affected the ways in which their diets have changed since Asian cuisine has effectively become a staple of the Australian food landscape. Meanwhile, for a course in the Communication Strand called Communication and Social Relations which enrols 500 students, for instance, the week we learn about gender in the media, students at lectures view both still and moving images of hyper-masculinity and hyper-feminity through examples from film (e.g. Hollywood and Asian cinemas) and television (Australian soaps and advertisements), while in the week we learn about the topical issue of multiculturalism in Australia, we go on a field trip during tutorials to the Immigration Museum. At the Immigration Museum, students are tasked with choosing an artefact in order to reflect on it as the first written assignment.

Students from Communication Debates and Approaches, another Communication Strand course, which often sees no less than 300 students enrolled, choose an artefact from the Australian indigenous cultures exhibition at the Melbourne Museum and reflect about it as their first assignment in order to understand how indigenous identities are expressed and assessed through art. I also engage local Australian indigenous artists to talk to students about their work in the context of providing them the example of the indigenous voice through the creative industry. Such topics allow Media and Communication students who will be public relations practitioners, journalists, advertisers, filmmakers, television producers and designers, just to name a few, start to understand the complex issues around them. They will, after all, engage with such issues in one way or another in their chosen professions. A critical engagement with such real-world issues fulfils the objectives of these Communication Strand courses and thus maintains quality assurance standards. Moreover, themes involving the study of Australian indigenous cultures also allow international students an opportunity to engage with the cultural heritage of their host nation.

Maintaining quality assurance standards in courses can be made more enjoyable through interaction between teaching stuff and students. My lectures and tutorials are very interactive as students are asked to respond to the material I present to them within the framework of the concepts introduced to them. In Sex and Gender in Asia (AMC Major), for instance, students learn that gender and sexuality are complex rather than simply falling into the heterosexual normative. So I dedicate a week to discussing the transgendered *kathoey* of Thailand with a role playing activity to help students understand the experiences of the liminal sex. Since my students come from Australian and international backgrounds, I try to make my lectures more interesting. For instance, when we discussed indigenous Australian issues in Communication and Social Relations, I invited an indigenous elder to give the lecture. However, I ran the lecture like a talk show by interviewing him about growing up as an Australian indigenous person. Also, knowing that students come from a variety of programmes and countries, the artefacts I use primarily come from Australia, Asia and North America in order for the courses to be relevant to both the Australian context as well as an international one. Hence, at different stages in the courses, students are able to identify and recognize the artefacts while interrogating them critically from thematic perspectives. They also learn new material that takes the form of being introduced to new and different cultures and societies. The lack of appreciation of new and different cultures and societies, however, takes a disturbing turn outside the classroom. While Australia has had decades of experience with international students, it needs to recognize that there are certain prejudices that the community holds towards them.

Stereotyping International Students

When the draft strategy was first published in April 2015, I wrote an opinion piece for the online news site *The Conversation* (Gomes 2015a). The comments section soon started to fill up with comments from readers—many claiming to have direct or indirect experiences with international students in the classroom as fellow (local) students, as instructors with international students in their classes or as friends/relatives of such instructors—pointing to how expanding international education would contribute to the declining standards of the university classroom and how because of that the quality of the Australian degree would propel downwards since universities would have to "dumb down" their courses. The basic theme of the comments was that international students are not on equal footing as local students primarily because of their poor English-language skills.

In April 2015, the Australian Broadcasting Corporation (ABC) aired a *Four Corners* programme with the title "Degrees of Deception" that turned the spotlight on international education and international students in Australia a few weeks after the release of the strategy (Besser 2015). The programme alleged that not only was international education fraught with underhanded and dishonest practice, but that international students were ill-equipped to study in Australia primarily because of poor English-language skills, which led them to resorting to cheating through plagiarism. The programme also claimed that international students are coming to Australia as permanent residence (PR) hunters rather as legitimate students. Interviewed for the programme were former academics and casual academic staff who claimed that they were being forced by their universities to pass international students even though they were not up to standard. While *Four Corners* is an investigative programme that specializes in exposès, it instigated a swarm of comments on its Facebook page which generally blamed international students for bringing down standards in the classroom, with a number of these comments coming from members of the public claiming to teach at universities.

International Students Are More Than Just Bad English Speakers and PR Hunters

While the *Four Corners* programme, the resulting public comments on its Facebook page, as well as the comments from my *The Conversation* article emphasized international students as nothing more than hapless victims struggling with a foreign language, I see international students as having the potential to be empowered individuals. In my own research I see international students consistently making the effort to improve their English communication skills and provide avenues to improve their abilities in this area. As a male undergraduate respondent from China explains:

> I try to talk with [Australians] but maybe because my English very poor so I can't communicate very well. I… just think I need to improve my English skill and try to talk with them [so that I] …feel suited [to living in]… Australia.

For this student, learning English is paramount so that he is able to communicate with locals and hence feel that Australia is home for him. A number of respondents told me that they do try to improve their English-speaking skills by talking to other international students in English and by engaging in English-language entertainment and news programmes which they access online. In other words, they consciously turn to Hollywood films and television shows as well as to international online news websites such as the BBC and CNN in order to improve their English-speaking skills.

International students are aware that having a good command of the English language means that they are arming themselves with the necessary skills to face the global workplace. Rather than merely being hungry for PR, international students are to a significant degree international actors who consider their transient experiences in Australia as adding to their ever evolving cosmopolitanism and contributing to the internationalization of their host nation (Gomes 2015b). Here I noticed that there is a new and emerging trend among international students that places global mobility at the heart of these transient migrants. In other words, international students in Australia hold aspirations for transnational mobility with ambitions to live and work in the big cities of Europe, North America and Asia, with returning to the home nation a possibly in the future. This aspirational mobility is encouraged by their experiences in Australia in terms of their ability to form friendship networks with fellow international students and their sense of belonging to the home nation provided by rapid developments in communication and media technologies.

A possible reason why international students are stereotyped in Australia could be because of their lack of friendships with locals, particularly domestic students.

Lack of Local Friends

In 2013, I conducted 60 face-to-face interviews with international students in Melbourne, most of whom were of Asian heritage. The findings revealed that international students strongly adhere to that identity and form a parallel multinational society made up of fellow international students that has very few "external" connections to Australian society. International students in this study note that their visa status allows them to not only identify with each other but also provide emotional and practical support. Here they explain that only other international students will understand the challenges they face as foreign students, for example, loneliness and cultural shocks. They further note that only fellow international students will be able to assist them with the practical issues connected with being a foreigner, for example, opening bank accounts and finding grocery stores that stock the food they are used to—issues they explain that local students do not face. Unfortunately, limiting social networks to only include other international students also prevents meaningful relationships being formed with locals, particularly domestic students. A female undergraduate from Singapore explains:

> I feel like students—local students—don't really mix much with Asian[s], except for local Asians they will mix around, but not Asian-Asian.

Clearly, the international students surveyed here are concerned about their lack of local friends, which perhaps prevents them from feeling socially connected, content and satisfied in the host nation (Hendrickson et al. 2011). Those who do count Australians as friends note that they had to actively get to know locals while at the same time developing and maintaining relationships with other international students. The participants generally state that while they would like to be friends with Australians, they feel that there are barriers to this from taking place. These include a lack of understanding of the Asian cultures the international students come from and the issues that international students encounter while in Australia (e.g. homesickness and accommodation problems) as well as language differences. The participants are resigned to the notion that the difficulties they have in speaking not only English but Australian English fluently are to blame for their lack of local friends. While researchers often point out that language is a barrier for the formation of intercultural relationships with members of the host nation (Gudykunst et al. 1991; Yamazaki et al. 1997; Kudo and Simkin 2003), the results of my research point out that some students are taking matters in their own hands (so to speak) to remedy this situation by improving their English-language skills.

Perception That Australians Are White and the Inability to Connect with Asian-Australians

While the majority of the participants have been in Australia for more than six months, many of them have conventional ideas about Australians as being only "white" and lack the conceptual means to differentiate that concept. The international student participants are able to see that they exist in a multicultural society made up of other international students from the homeland, region and sometimes elsewhere, yet many of them read Australian society as made up almost completely of Caucasians. To them, an Australian friend is a white Australian friend. This notion of the Australian local population being white is not surprising since the dominant discourse in Australia is based on an Anglo-Celtic British history and culture (Hage 1998; Stratton 1999), and its local entertainment and news media are strongly dominated by white faces (Jakubowicz and Seneviratne 1996).

At the same time, some of the participants, particularly those from Asia, do acknowledge that there is an Asian-Australian community, yet they also racialize this community with participants stating that their understanding of Asian-Australian is Australian-born Chinese or, as they explain, "ABCs". Those who say that they have Asian-Australian friends state that they are new permanent residents, while others explain that the ABCs only want to be friends with white Australians and not with them. Some participants provide the explanation that ABCs are more Australian than Asian and hence have more in common with white Australians than they do with Asian international students. However, the international students I spoke to also do not identify with Asian-Australian issues such as the now and again discussions in the media about the lack of diversity on Australian television. While the participants come from Asia, they find it challenging to identify with Asian-Australians and Asian-Australian issues because of the fundamental differences in direct circumstance and experience.

Conclusion

While the *National Strategy for International Education 2025* is an excellent indicator of the value the Australian government places on international education and the recognition of international students in the broader contexts of cultural exchange and future professional developments for Australia, the strategy's aspirations to expand the international education industry will pose certain challenges for institutions in terms of managing culturally diverse student bodies. In this chapter, I have suggested that rather than looking at increasing diversity on institutional campuses because of larger numbers of international students as a difficult issue to confront, such diversity instead provides an incentive for curriculum development. However, I also highlight the conundrum presented by the presence on international students in Australia. While international students have had an increasing presence in Australia since the 1950s, which accelerated from the 1980s onwards, the broader Australian community still has conventional and relatively uninformed notions about them, with a possible reason being the lack of connections between international students and local students. Perhaps the continuing and persistent incorporation of both global and local examples in courses and the active use of strategies to incorporate interaction in the classroom might help reduce the disconnections between international students from Australian society while allowing local students to gain a better understanding of the cultures and societies international students come from.

Acknowledgements Dr. Catherine Gomes is the recipient of an Australian Research Council DECRA Fellowship (project number DE130100551). She also receives funding from RMIT University.

NOTE

1. While Australia is also host to students on exchange/study abroad, this chapter does not include them under the banner of "international students". International students in this chapter are full-fee-paying students. In other words, their education in Australia is not subsidized by the Australian government as it is for local students. Largely international students fund their education in Australia through private means. Some students might be funded by scholarships from their home nations or by Australian programmes such as the Australian Agency for International Development and International Postgraduate Research Scholarships scholarships.

REFERENCES

Arkoudis, S., Yu, X., Baik, C., Borland, H., Chang, S., Lang, I., Lang, J., Pearce, P., & Watty, K. (2010). *Finding common ground: Enhancing interaction between domestic and international students*. Australian Learning and Teaching Council. Available online at: http://www.cshe.unimelb.edu.au/research/projectsites/enhancing_interact.html.

Australian Bureau of Statistics. (2011). *International Students*, 13 October 2013. http://www.abs.gov.au/ausstats/abs@.nsf/Lookup/4102.0Main+Features20 Dec+2011

Australian Bureau of Statistics. (2013, July). *Australian social trends*, viewed 21 July 2014. http://www.abs.gov.au/AUSSTATS/abs@.nsf/Lookup/4102.0M ain+Features20July+2013#p6

Australian Department of Education and Training. (2015). *International education in Australia, 1994–2015*. Department of Education and Training Media Centre. Available online at: https://internationaleducation.gov.au/research/International-Student-Data/Pages/InternationalStudentData2015.aspx.

Australian Department of Education and Training. (2016). Research snapshot: International student numbers 2015. Available online at: https://internationaleducation.gov.au/research/Research-Snapshots/Documents/Student%20 Numbers%202015.pdf.

Australian Government. (2015). Draft national strategy for international education: For consultation. Available online at: https://internationaleducation.gov.au/International-network/Australia/InternationalStrategy/Documents/Draft%20National%20Strategy%20for%20International%20Education.pdf.

Australian Government. (2016). National Strategy for International Education 2025. Available online at https://nsie.education.gov.au/sites/nsie/files/docs/national_strategy_for_international_education_2025.pdf.

Australian Trade Commission. (2016). *Education costs in Australia*, viewed 7 January 2016. http://www.studyinaustralia.gov.au/global/australian-education/education-costs

Besser, L. (2015, April 20). Degrees of deception. *Four Corners*. Melbourne: Australian Broadcasting Corporation.

Department of Foreign Affairs and Training. (2016). New Colombo Plan. Available online at: http://dfat.gov.au/people-to-people/new-colombo-plan/pages/new-colombo-plan.aspx.

Department of Immigration and Border Protection, Australia. (2014). *Work conditions for Student visa holders*, viewed 20 July 2014. http://www.immi.gov.au/students/students/working_while_studying

Gomes, C. (2015a). International student report emphasizes their value, but not the means. *The Conversation*. Available online at: https://theconversation.com/

international-student-report-emphasises-their-value-but-not-the-means-39626#comment_637156.

Gomes, C. (2015b). Where to next after graduation?: International students in Australia and their aspirations for transnational mobility. Special Edition. *Crossings: Journal of Migration and Culture, 6*(1), 41–58.

Gudykunst, W. B., Gao, G., Sudweeks, S., Ting-Toomey, S., & Nishida, T. (1991). Themes in opposite sex, Japanese-North American relationships. In S. Ting-Toomey & F. Korzenny (Eds.), *Cross-cultural interpersonal communication*. Newbury Park: Sage.

Hage, G. (1998). *White nation; fantasies of white supremacy in a multicultural society*. New York: Routledge.

Hendrickson, B., Rosen, D., & Aune, R. K. (2011). An analysis of friendship networks, social connectedness, homesickness, and satisfaction levels of international students. *International Journal of Intercultural Relations, 35*(3), 281–295.

Hughes, J. (2015, October 15). Malaysia seeks 200,000 international students by 2020. *Masterstudies.com*. Available online at: http://www.masterstudies.com/news/Malaysia-Seeks-200-000-International-Students-by-2020-495/.

Jakubowicz, A., & Seneviratne, K. (1996). Ethnic conflict and the Australian media. *Making Multicultural Australia*. Available online at: http://www.multiculturalaustralia.edu.au/doc/jakubowicz_3.pdf.

Kudo, K., & Simkin, K. A. (2003). Intercultural friendship formation: The case of Japanese students at an Australian university. *Journal of Intercultural Studies, 24*, 91–114.

McLoughlin, C., & Lee, M. J. W. (2009). *Personalized learning spaces and self-regulated learning: Global examples of effective pedagogy*. Proceedings ascilite Auckland 2009. Available online at: http://citeseerx.ist.psu.edu/viewdoc/download?doi=10.1.1.412.857&rep=rep1&type=pdf.

Stratton, J. (1999). Multiculturalism and the whitening machine, or how Australians become white. In G. Hage & R. Couch (Eds.), *The future of Australian multiculturalism: Reflections on the twentieth anniversary of Jean Martins The migrant presence* (pp. 163–188). Sydney: University of Sydney.

Student Services, The University of Melbourne. (2016). Financial aid. Available online at: http://services.unimelb.edu.au/finaid/planning/cost_of_living/summary.

UNESCO. (2016). Global flow of tertiary-level students. Montreal: UNESCO: *Institute for Statistics*. Available online at: http://www.uis.unesco.org/Education/Pages/international-student-flow-viz.aspx.

Yamazaki, M., Taira, N., Shun-ya, N., & Yokoyama, T. (1997). The role of ethnicity in the development of the Asian students' attitudes toward Japanese and other cultures. *Japanese Journal of Educational Psychology, 45*, 119–131.

CHAPTER 11

Conclusion: When All Is Said and Done

Deane E. Neubauer and Catherine Gomes

INTRODUCTION

The chapters in this volume repeatedly demonstrate that efforts to "pin down" quality across a variety of academic settings and organizational processes are fraught with difficulty. In their chapter on quality assurance and quality culture in Malaysia, Fauza Ab. Ghaffar and A. Abrizah, for instance, comment that there is simply no commonly accepted notion of quality in higher education. In other words, as we point out in the introduction to this volume, what one accepts as the definition of quality as well as the central meanings of the term, is largely dependent on the circumstances and settings within which this notion of quality is applied. Our illustrative chapters in this volume sought to focus on a particular intersect that arises when one moves from the level of national or regional quality assurance to that of discrete institutional circumstances. As one can attest, this exercise allows readers to discern common elements that

D.E. Neubauer (✉)
East-West Center, University of Hawaii,
Honolulu, HI, USA

C. Gomes
School of Media and Communication, RMIT University,
Melbourne, Australia

© The Author(s) 2017
D.E. Neubauer, C. Gomes (eds.),
Quality Assurance in Asia-Pacific Universities,
DOI 10.1007/978-3-319-46109-0_11

arise surrounding the issue of quality as complex higher education institutions (HEIs) organize themselves around different purposes, situate themselves significantly in different cultures, and respond to a complex array of political, economical and social circumstances as they seek to comprehend quality within this range of variance. Institutions thus face the challenge to develop disciplined yet creative means for students, faculty and administrative structures to confidently hold legitimate representation of quality in these particular circumstances. It is our view that this sample of chapters provides a rich and useful array of different and creative ways particular institutions both struggle and succeed in developing meaningful approaches to quality.

One is prone to inquire, however, as to whether there may be a useful step beyond these exercises. Is it possible to generate a discourse for higher education quality that serves the institution at the organizational level, where much of the regulatory exercise of quality assurance within higher education takes place? Can this be done while still providing institutions with sufficient flexibility and reach and while also taking into context idiosyncratic differences of individual variance?

This, as it turns out, is very close to the question that the Council on Higher Education Accreditation (CHEA) in the USA not long ago put to its International Advisory Group (IAG).[1] With an individual membership that includes some kind of association with many of the major national and international quality-assurance organizations, the IAG sought not to engage in yet another effort to specify which standards of quality assurance might prove to be "basic", "essential" or "irreducible" to any disciplined effort at quality assurance. Instead, the IAG chose to look "behind" any such itemization of standards and ask whether one *could* identify a set of common *principles* that might underlie both national and international quality-assurance specifications. In May 2015, the CHEA unveiled the result of this several years-long effort at identification and specification of these common quality-assurance principles. (CHEA 2015). In the remainder of this chapter, we will look at each of these principles identified and articulated by the CHEA in the context of this volume as we seek to better understand how quality activities at the institutional level can contribute toward meeting the intent of quality-assurance standards promulgated at the regulatory level (across the very considerable differences of country and region).

QUALITY PRINCIPLES

Principle One *Quality and higher education providers: Assuring and achieving quality in higher education is the primary responsibility of higher education providers and their staff.*

Within quality discourses this idea of quality assurance as the responsibility of institutions and their staff is often translated as: quality is everybody's business! This simple bromide appears so immediately self-evident that it is seemingly difficult to comprehend how one could disagree with it. However, it is through an examination of institutions that we find evidence that at the operational level practitioners at all levels **do not** self-consciously "engage" quality in their activities. By practitioners, we refer to individuals and groups involved within a variety of university settings such as classrooms, administration, research and so on. They may assume that their activities (almost by definition) are representative of quality, but quality <u>per se</u> is often perceived as those activities that are defined elsewhere: either by a higher level of administration, or more usually by some external entity explicitly charged with the identification and determination of quality, either at the regional, national or international levels, or by professional identification and certification. Within such a received culture, quality comes to be *represented* by whatever definitions, measures and procedures such entities embrace and extend for their activities. Ironically, much of the operational definitions of quality are expropriated by such external entities and measures. Thus within institutions, cultures of quality come to be assumed to reside within everyday activity, but tend to lose their discursive place within the institution itself. The exception, of course, is when particular notions of quality are attached to formal internal procedures such as course evaluations, criteria for promotion and tenure, and so on.

Our point is that the externalization of formal assessments bifurcates both informal and formal cultures of quality in ways that ironically may de-sensitize faculty, staff, students, researchers, administrators—and indeed all participants—from what might be viewed as essential elements of quality within the higher education process.

Principle Two *Quality and students: The education provided to students must always be of high quality whatever the learning outcomes pursued.*

Again, as in the case with Principle One, to assert the above would appear to articulate a self-conscious redundancy. However, considerable evidence exists within the quality-assurance literature itself which paradoxically and ironically asserts that the imposition of learning outcomes within a curriculum can and does at times lead to situations in which quality may actually decline. For instance in the USA, this paradigm begins in K-12 where mandatory testing becomes the default learning outcome, and overall quality within the classroom declines as instructors "teach to the test". An analogy exists within higher education as quality-assurance entities and university central administrations develop discrete metrics such as key performance indicators (KPIs) to assess personnel in a process that leads to crafting classroom and other faculty behavior around "making the KPIs". This leads to behaviors which on other dimensions may be viewed as detracting from rather than adding to high quality (see, e.g. Ghaffar and Abriah's review of the University of Malaya in Chap. 8).

This situation may also be likened to the role that rankings can come to play within higher education behavior. The ostensible purpose of a rankings culture is to provide an empirical indicator or set of indicators that results in the rank order arrangement of HEIs precisely so that one can make a determination quickly from a single summary datum of the relative quality status of one institution relative to another, or to others. Within this process, rankings are necessarily highly *reductionist* in the sense that to provide such a summative indicator, it is necessary to ignore a wide range of alternative data/information. Thus, of necessity, rankings ostensibly based on quality must distort the overall data relevant to an institution——an issue we raise in Chap. 1 where we reference work by Marginson and Sawir 2005; Liu 2011; and Neubauer 2011. In this context, the burden of this quality principle is that HEIs of all types must guard against whatever outcome measures they develop and so risk becoming reductionist at the expense of other, more complex notions and understandings of quality.

Principle Three *Quality and society: The quality of higher education provision is judged by how well it meets the needs of society, engenders public confidence and sustains public trust.*

The burden of this quality principle for HEIs varies with time, place and the social, economic and political climate within which they operate. Within the contemporary social and economic climate in which all of the institutions featured in this volume are operating, a common complaint about/against higher education in general and its institutions is the inability of graduates to find sufficient or appropriate employment upon graduation. This situation is viewed by virtually all involved as clearly exemplary of the language in principal three of "meets the needs of society, engenders public confidence and sustains public trust." Whether in the USA, Japan, Australia, China, Malaysia, Taiwan or Vietnam, the inability of large numbers of higher education graduates to find suitable employment is held in large part to be a distinct failing of higher education as a social practice and as an overall failing of quality, broadly conceived.

However, as a variety of commentators have pointed out, to so readily reach such a conclusion and to impune quality overall as a result is not fully justified. Peter Hershock (2012), for example, has usefully linked the role that higher education increasing plays within the overall global economy as akin to a structural dilemma which has beset it. Here, Hersock notes that the global economy directly engages higher education by creating expectations for the qualitative attributes of its graduates. It does this, however, almost exclusively outside the influence pattern of higher education. In short, higher education is held responsible for being able to meet the employment demands of the global economy and its impacts on any local economy but is not provided the means and the capability for graduates to effectively engage with that economy in order to shape how such needs will be developed and expressed. The most that HEIs can do is to be move forward by seeking to revise and modify their curricula, teaching methods and hiring practices in order to anticipate such changes.[2]

Principle Four *Quality and government: Governments have a role in encouraging and supporting quality higher education.*

The apparent self-evident nature of this principle is such that many might be tempted to disregard its overall relevance. Indeed, during past decades, government has played a major role in the massification of education. As a powerful ideology, the growth and spread of neo-liberalism has led to a more restrained posture on the part of the public sector in its support of higher education. In the context of the global recession of 2008, and the pressure it placed on governmental budgets throughout the world, spending within the public sector for higher education suffered a major shock. In this regard at least, one can say that government support for higher education has been significantly challenged. Yet across such a broad front, government must be seen to have affected the ability of HEIs to create, extend and maintain quality.

Finance, of course, is not the only way that governmental activity affects quality. It can certainly be argued that over the past several decades, government has been very active at a regulatory level in its effort to provide the mechanisms of quality which can be appropriately advanced though this sector, most specifically through the bureaucratic mechanisms of quality assurance themselves. It is in this arena that it is useful to be aware of the considerable diversity that exists within governmental regulation of higher education quality, and the case that can be made that in some countries the process certainly proceeds more successfully than in others, and is among other things, a major vector for how the sector experiences or is protected from the ravages of corruption and various aspects of bureaucratic mismanagement (e.g. the commonly acknowledged cases of Vietnam, India and others).[3]

Principle V *Quality and accountability: It is the responsibility of higher education providers and quality assurance and accreditation bodies to sustain a strong commitment to accountability and provide regular evidence of quality.*

This is probably the most commonly recognized principle of higher education quality assurance. Yet, as the various chapters of this volume suggest it is far from a self-evident case that how such "regular evidence" of quality and a strong commitment to quality is itself intrinsic to how HEIs and QA agencies engage in such activity. All HEIs in all countries *at some level* will be challenged as to how to "provide regular evidence of quality", especially when one raises the question of "to whom" is such evidence to be provided. In the USA, for example, higher education accreditation has gone through a great deal of controversy in the past 15 years. This is due in large part to the question of just how "transparent" HEIs should be, especially when providing evidence of learning outcomes for students (see, e.g. the US case as summarized by Provezis in a relatively early stage in the debate. 2010).

The issue of how to "provide regular evidence of quality" has particular relevance within the developmental dynamics of Asian higher education–to which some of our sample institutions featured in this volume partake. By looking at Asian institutions, the authors point to the ability of institutions and societies to frame, value and exchange higher education quality through the complicated process known as mutual recognition. Here authors point to the willingness of institutions within one society to rec-ognize and accept a definition of quality as expressed in various currencies, e.g. course credits, grade levels, degrees, such that another society will accept those at equal value. This process stands at the center of the phe-nomenon of cross-border education, an arena in which an increasing num-ber of societies are dependent on education for income while still seeking to maintain their higher education systems at current levels (an issue that is especially critical in the "low demographic" countries of Taiwan, Japan and Korea, e.g.). Mutual recognition is at the core of what international higher education quality-assurance networks and societies are striving to accomplish; to provide a useful "currency" within which multinational higher education systems may exchange for their mutual benefit, and as a process has been a major initiative of UNESCO for the past four decades.[4]

One central element of quality assurance to which the essays in this volume attest is that at the institutional level their translation into the complex practices of higher education make up the data on which mutual recognition as a process is based. Without some form of common frame of reference to act as a counter balance a dynamic tends to exist that appears throughout higher education to "define" any "standard" relevant to higher education largely by the extant local practices (from the presump-tion that quality inheres to the locally relevant set of practices), or absent that, to treat any such standard as of some distant relevance far removed from the local. It is in its capacity to embed standards and notions of practice in presumptions of quality principles that makes accreditation and quality assurance of such value when they are able to provide bridges not only across complex and differing institutional practices at local levels but as languages of a common higher education culture that can exist, as is increasingly the case, across regions as well and through the com-plexities of national differentiation. It is difficult to perceive how mutual recognition, on which cross-border education is increasingly dependent could otherwise go forward with anything like the scale that it has already achieved and to the levels currently predicted for it in the neighborhood of 7 million in 2020 (on this see Hudzik and Stohl 2012).

Principle Six *Quality and the role of quality assurance and accreditation bodies: Quality assurance and accreditation bodies, working with higher edu-cation providers and their leadership, staff and students, are responsible for the implementation of processes, tools, benchmarks and measures of learning outcomes that help to create a shared understanding of quality.*

Perhaps the most important way in which quality assurance and accreditation bodies can work effectively with higher education providers in order to ensure that quality standards are met is through clear and direct communication. A challenge which various chapters in this volume point to is the menagerie of quality assurance and accreditation bodies they have to deal with at the international, national and institutional levels. Because of the various levels of bureaucracy involved in interpreting quality frameworks that higher education providers have to deal with, better ways of streamlining communication between all parties involved need to be set in place. Here, not only does information from quality assurance and accreditation bodies about the standards required from industry need to be clearly mapped out and available, but these bodies must also collaborate with institutions to form these frameworks. A top-down approach from quality assurance and accreditation bodies, in other words, should not be the norm. Instead these bodies should work collaboratively with institutions, particularly those that are research-active in order to develop strategies and new directions for not only maintaining but also developing new benchmarks for quality. In Chap. 3, for instance, Dhanatya illustrates a useful context in which the impact and necessity of research on quality standards may be expanded.

Principle Seven *Quality and change: Quality higher education needs to be flexible, creative and innovative; developing and evolving to meet students' needs, to justify the confidence of society and to maintain diversity.*

The higher education sector worldwide has undergone considerable change over the past three decades. This is due not only to significant changes that directly impact the sector, but also to the generalized impact of global factors that influence daily life. In particular, we highlight here the unprecedented growth of international education and the rise of the digital age that have changed classroom dynamics and modes of learning. Higher education providers have had to meet these challenges head-on while still finding ways to maintain quality standards. However, as Gomes points out, in Chap. 10, in her discussion of nationally and culturally diverse cohorts, these challenges can have positive outcomes in terms of internationalizing the curriculum in her example of teaching in an Australian institution.

International education has become a popular and lucrative business model for HEIs particularly in the English-speaking West. The UK and Australia, for instance, have experienced decreasing government funding for teaching and research and thus have had to change their business and education models to meet this challenge. Hence, the rise of international education where countries such as the UK and Australia, as well as the USA, Canada and New Zealand invest time and energy to attract full-fee paying international students who pay higher fees that their domestic counterparts. The result is very diverse cohorts of both domestic and international students whose learning styles differ from each other. Instructors at HEIs often struggle in their efforts to effectively teach such cohorts especially since there is little homogeneity in terms of educational, cultural and societal backgrounds. However, rather than seeing this as a difficult challenge, institutions can harness this situation in order to internationalize their curriculum and bring intercultural learnings into the classroom. Graduating students after all will be part of a global workforce where international mobility (Gomes 2016) and collaboration are the norm.

We now live in a polymedia age (Madianou and Miller 2011), where communication of information and connectivity are determined and navigated by rapid improvements in digital media and communication technologies. Students who enter HEIs are not only digitally literate, but also juggle multiple digital platforms and mobile devices with almost all of them not knowing a time before the Internet. Hence, the ways by which they learn are increasingly tied to their expertise in navigating digital spaces. Likewise, employers are constantly and rapidly changing their modes of operation, and so expect work-ready graduates who are themselves able to adapt to ever-changing digital spaces. Yet at the same time, employers expect graduates to have basic entry-level knowledge and skills of the industry that they enter. For example, a teacher must have a dynamic understanding of education pedagogies which can only be realized through learning (from instructors), experience (through placement), sharing and discussion (with instructors, course mates and mentors during placement) and self-reflection. The challenge for HEIs is to balance a creative and flexible blended form of learning that harnesses the power of digital spaces while being comprehensive to meet the ever-changing needs of industry. At the same time, higher education providers need to realize that students have varying degrees of digital literacy which are highly culturally specific (Chang and Gomes, 2017). In a classroom of both domestic and international students, there will be of apparent necessity, different forms of digital literacy. Institutions thus need to exert one or more forms of blended learning that are flexible enough to incorporate these different digital learning styles which then have benefits all learners as part of the agenda for internationalizing the curriculum.

CONCLUSION

As is often the case in life, in this instance, "both things" as it were "are true"—by which we mean that quality within higher education environments must necessarily subscribe to basic quality principles (in order to frame any kind of possible basis for agreement, exchange, debates over relative currencies of value, etc.) *and* seek understandings of and pursue manifestations of quality that are sensitive to the nature of local cultures of quality and pathways to complex understandings of value. The result of this continuous engagement is a dynamic in which efforts to pursue quality again necessarily involve some form of continuous interaction with systemic relevant standards and criteria such as those developed by accreditation and quality-assurance entities and the always particularistic nature of "local environments" whether these take the form of the oldest and most statused institutions in a higher education system or relatively new institutions, perhaps invented to address new and emergent challenges in the information/knowledge society of which we are all so much a part. The burden of this chapter is to underscore the effort engaged in by the Advisory Group to recognize and accept the extraordinary differentiation present within complexly different higher education settings and to seek out and establish a set of principles that can guide and inform efforts to create both effective evaluation and the basis for comparability

NOTES

1. In the spirit of full disclosure, Deane Neubauer was a member of this 20+ member advisory group that represented participants from throughout the world.
2. See, for example, Standard Four of the Handbook of the WASC Senior College and University Commission of the USA which states: **Standard 4: Creating an Organization Committed to Quality Assurance, Institutional Learning, and Improvement.**
    "The institution engages in sustained, evidence-based, and participatory self-reflection about how effectively it is accomplishing its purposes and achieving its educational objectives. The institution considers the changing environment of higher education in envisioning its future. These activities inform both institutional planning and systematic evaluations of educational effectiveness. The results of institutional inquiry, research, and data collection are used to

establish priorities, to plan, and to improve quality and effectiveness." And substandards: 4.6: "The institution periodically engages its multiple constituencies, including the governing board, faculty, staff and others in institutional reflection and planning processes that are based on the examination of data and evidence. These processes assess the institution's strategic position, articulate priorities, examine the alignment of its purposes, core functions, and resources, and define the future direction of the institution…" And 4.7: "Within the context of its mission and structural and financial realities, the institution considers changes that are currently taking place and are anticipated to take place within the institution and higher education environment as part of its planning, new program development and resource allocation" (WASC 2016).

3. Note, for example, the recent treatment of this by Rui Yang: "An academic culture that is based on meritocratic values, free enquiry and competition is largely absent in East Asia. Throughout the region, academic dishonesty has long been an issue, from students cheating to fraud by scientists. Research shows that academic dishonesty is increasing in Hong Kong and Taiwan. South Koreans dub their nation the 'Republic of Plagiarism'." 2016.

4. For an overall exemplification of the process, see UNESCO 2007.

REFERENCES

Chang, S., & Gomes, C. (2017). Digital journeys: A perspective on understanding the digital experiences of international students. *Journal of International Students, 7*(2), 347–366.

Council on Higher Education Accreditation (CHEA). (2015). The CIQG international quality principles: Toward a shared understanding of quality. S. Uvalić-Trumbić (Ed.). Available at: http://www.chea.org/pdf/Principles_Papers_Complete_web.pdf. Accessed 9 June 2016.

Gomes, C. (2016). *Transient mobility and middle class identity: Media and migration in Australia and Singapore.* New York: Palgrave Macmillan.

Hershock, P. (2012). Information and innovation in a global knowledge society: Implications for higher education. In D. Neubauer (Ed.), *The emergent knowledge society and the future of higher education: Asian perspectives* (pp. 7–25). New York: Routledge.

Hudzik, J. K., & Stohl, M. (2012). Comprehensive and strategic internationalization of U.S. higher education. In D. K. Dardorff, H. de Wit, & J. D. Heyl (Eds.), *The SAGE handbook of international higher education.* Los Angeles: SAGE.

Liu, N. C. (2011). The phenomenon of academic ranking of universities model: Future directions. In *Quality in higher education*, co-editor with J. Hawkins & T. DeMott. Available at: http://publications.apec.org/publication-detail. php?pub_id=1204: August 2011. Accessed 10 June 2016.

Madianou, M., & Miller, D. (2011). Mobile phone parenting: Reconfiguring relationships between Filipina migrant mothers and their left-behind children. *New Media & Society, 13*(3), 457–470.

Marginson, S., & Sawir, E. (2005). Interrogating global flows in higher education. *Globalization, Societies and Education, 3*(3), 281–309.

Neubauer, D. (2011). How might university rankings contribute to quality assurance endeavors? In *Quality in Higher Education*, co-editor with J. Hawkins & T. DeMott. Available at: http://publications.apec.org/publication-detail. php?pub_id=1204: Accessed 10 June 2016.

Provezis, S. (2010). *Regional accreditation and student learning outcomes: Mapping the territory.* Institute for Learning Outcomes Assessment. Available at: http://www.learningoutcomesassessment.org/documents/Provezis.pdf. Accessed 10 June 2016.

UNESCO. (2007). The regional convention on the recognition of studies, diplomas and degrees in higher education in Asia and the Pacific. Kunming, People's Republic of China, May 24–25, 2005.

WASC Senior College and University Commission. (2016). *Handbook of accreditation 2013 revised.* Available at: https://www.wascsenior.org/resources/ handbook-accreditation-2013. Accessed 2 Sept 2016.

Yang, R. (2016). Corruption undermines rise of East Asian universities. *University World News,* Issue 00416, 11 June. Available at: http://www.universityworld-news.com/article.php?story=20160126130528586. Accessed 11 June 2016.

INDEX

Note: Page numbers followed by 'n' denote notes.

© The Author(s) 2017

D.E. Neubauer, C. Gomes (eds.),
Quality Assurance in Asia-Pacific Universities,
DOI 10.1007/978-3-319-46109-0